C o n t e n t s

KEY TO MAPS

✈ Airport

⭐ Start of walk

Ⓜ Metro

Introduction

Samuel Johnson said that anyone who tires of London must be weary of life itself. The same is true of Amsterdam: a seductive and entertaining city made all the more attractive by its manageable size and easy-going atmosphere, Amsterdam combines big city attractions with the character of an overgrown village.

Packed into an area small enough to cross on foot in under half an hour are some 40 museums, over 70 theatres and almost 150 art galleries. The city is home to two internationally renowned orchestras, as well as the Dutch national ballet and opera companies. Yet it has none of the stress, hype or tension of a big metropolis: bicycles are more numerous than cars, there are scores of congenial cafés where even first-time visitors are welcomed as old friends and (with the exception of brash Kalverstraat) you will search hard to find a supermarket or chain store – Amsterdammers far prefer their traditional corner-shop grocery stores and specialist retailers.

Above all, Amsterdam is a lived-in city, not one devoted solely to tourism or commerce; after 5pm, when businesses close for the day, the streets throng with Amsterdammers, born and bred in the city, out for a walk or drinking with friends in pavement cafés, lending the city an almost Mediterranean atmosphere. Visitors to Amsterdam experience a living, vital city which Amsterdammers are proud to share – in the words of Nicolas Freeling, creator of the famous Dutch detective, Van der Valk – 'I know of no city where the outsider is so spontaneously taken to heart'.

'From my favourite spot on the floor I look up at the blue sky and the bare chestnut tree on whose branches little raindrops glisten like silver, and at the seagulls and other birds as they glide on the wind.'
ANNE FRANK

THOMAS COOK'S AMSTERDAM

Thomas Cook's first party to The Netherlands was organised in 1868. The following year he returned with a trip to the Amsterdam Exhibition. By 1899 Amsterdam was a regular feature of Cook's Tours. A brochure for that year advertised a conducted 'Easter tour to Holland and the Dead Cities of the Zuyder Zee', with first-class hotels and second-class travel, for £5 5s 0d. By then Thomas Cook had an office in Amsterdam, at 83 Damrak.

The 1911 brochure advertises carriages for a three-hour tour of the city, and a number of excursions including the island of Marken, Broek in Waterland ('the cleanest village in Holland' – which had no roads leading to it, for fear that horses would foul the streets), Edam and Zaandam, to see Peter the Great's cottage – still owned at the time by the Russian imperial family.

AMSTERDAM

BY

CHRISTOPHER CATLING

Produced by
Thomas Cook Publishing

Written by Christopher Catling
Updated by Mike Gerrard
Original photography by Ken Paterson
Original design by Laburnum Technologies Pvt Ltd

Editing and page layout by Cambridge Publishing
Management Ltd, Unit 2, Burr Elm Court,
Caldecote CB3 7NU
Series Editor: Karen Beaulah

Published by Thomas Cook Publishing
A division of Thomas Cook Tour Operations Ltd

PO Box 227, The Thomas Cook Business Park,
Units 15–16, Coningsby Road,
Peterborough PE3 8SB, United Kingdom
E-mail: books@thomascook.com
www.thomascookpublishing.com
Tel: +44 (0) 1733 416477

ISBN-13: 978-1-84157-546-9
ISBN-10: 1-84157-546-1

Text © 2006 Thomas Cook Publishing
Maps © 2006 Thomas Cook Publishing
Tram and Metro map © 2006 Communicarta Ltd

First edition © 2003 Thomas Cook Publishing
Second edition © 2006 Thomas Cook Publishing

Head of Thomas Cook Publishing: Chris Young
Project Editor: Linda Bass
Production/DTP Editor: Steven Collins

Printed and bound in Spain by: Grafo Industrias Gráficas, Basauri.

Cover design by: Liz Lyons Design, Oxford.
Front cover credits: Left © Robert Harding/Digital Vision; centre © Andre Jenny/Alamy;
right © PCL/Alamy
Back cover credits: Left © Corbis; right © Corbis

'Heroic, Resolute, Compassionate.'
The succinct motto on Amsterdam's
coat of arms.

'What impressed contemporaries about
Amsterdam was that it was a city entirely
dedicated to making money . . . all the
way up the Damrak the quay was
crammed with hoists, piles of
merchandise, porters and small ships
loading and unloading . . . almost the
whole world seemed to be assembled to
buy and sell.'
MARK GIROUARD

'The pungent salt smell, the northern,
maritime keynotes of seagull and herring,
the pointed brick buildings, tall and
narrow like herons, with their mosaic of
particoloured shutters, eaves, sills that give
the landscape their stiff, heraldic look . . .'
NICOLAS FREELING

'Amsterdam remains the refuge of all
those striving to free themselves from the
stifling atmosphere of small communities,
and that too forms part of the city's
strength and vitality.'
GEERT MAK

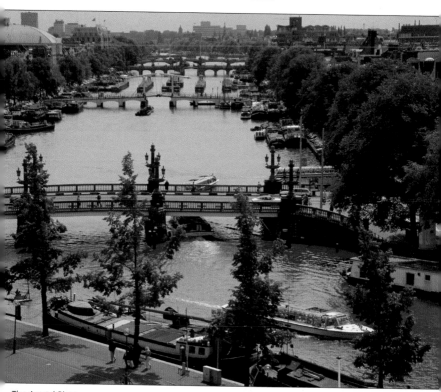

The Amstel River

The Land

Amsterdam, meaning 'Amstelledamme', or 'dam across the River Amstel', is the commercial capital of The Netherlands though, unusually, the Dutch parliament is based in The Hague. Visitors incorrectly refer to The Netherlands as Holland, which is like saying England instead of Britain. Holland consists of only the two western provinces along the North Sea: Noord (North) Holland, where Amsterdam is located though Haarlem is the provincial capital, and Zuid (South) Holland, where The Hague is located, which is both the provincial capital and the seat of government.

Deltawerken: the sea dominates the geography and history of The Netherlands

Nord and Zuid Holland, along with the province of Utrecht (capital, Utrecht) form a region known as the *Randstad*, meaning 'ring town', so-called because its cities form an almost circular conurbation. It is also known, more affectionately, as 'the big village', and it has a population of over 4 million – 27 per cent of the Dutch total of 14.8 million.

The *Randstad* is economically prosperous, accounting for almost half the country's total output. Amsterdam itself is an important banking and financial services centre. Around a third of the city's income comes from small businesses and the self-employed. Despite its laid-back atmosphere, the city is a hive of enterprise, with many people employed in computer consultancy, graphic design, journalism, publishing, architecture and the arts. Tourism and retailing are also major sources of revenue and employment.

The other cities of the *Randstad* include Rotterdam, the world's biggest port, Delft, Leiden and Gouda. Schiphol airport is also critical to the *Randstad* economy. Most visitors see it only as an efficient passenger airport but behind the scenes it has a huge freight-handling capacity and is a major distribution hub for European exports and imports – especially perishable goods, such as fruit, vegetables and cut flowers. Many of the exotic and out-of-season fruits that fill European supermarket shelves are flown into Schiphol from the Far East, Africa, the Caribbean and the Canary Islands for onward distribution by road.

This in turn has benefited the Dutch horticultural and agricultural industries. Much of the land to the south and west of Amsterdam is used for growing flowers, pot plants and greenhouse fruit and vegetables, such as tomatoes, peppers, cucumbers and strawberries. Tulip bulbs are the most famous product of the region but in terms of sales they actually rank fourth behind roses, chrysanthemums and carnations.

The bulb fields and gardens around Lisse, just south of Amsterdam, are a major tourist attraction in their own right, as is the world's largest daily flower auction at Aalsmeer, adjacent to Schiphol airport.

Much of the land around Amsterdam has been reclaimed over the centuries by constructing a complex system of dykes and dams to hold back the sea and drain the watery landscape. The resulting land is called polder, from *pol*, referring to the wooden poles or stakes that were originally used to stabilise the sides of the drainage dykes. Wind-powered mills were once used to raise the water through a series of ring canals, each one higher than the last, so that the water could eventually flow via natural rivers out to the sea. Nowadays the task of drainage is handled by electric pumps, but well-preserved windmills are still a characteristic feature of the Dutch landscape, especially to the north of Amsterdam, around Zaanse Schans.

The most recent area of polderisation lies immediately to the east of Amsterdam. The shallow IJsselmeer (formerly known as the Zuider Zee) was dammed in 1932 by building the 30-km *Afsluitdijk* (Enclosing Dyke). Part of the IJsselmeer was then drained to create Flevoland; this huge area of reclaimed land, measuring 1,800sq km, was officially declared the 12th province of The Netherlands in 1986. Today such large-scale polderisation schemes are surrounded by controversy. Environmentalists fear that further drainage of the IJsselmeer would damage a fragile ecology. Furthermore, if the water table falls below its present level, the wooden piles supporting Amsterdam's older buildings might dry out and rot, causing damage on a massive scale. To the relief of Amsterdam residents, further schemes have been put on hold and a temporary truce has been drawn in the elemental battle between the land and the sea.

A land reclaimed from the sea

History

1275	First documented reference to the city.
1300	First municipal charter, the town now creates and enforces its own laws.
1323	The town prospers on trade with England, Germany and the Baltic.
1345	Pilgrims flock to Amsterdam after a communion host thrown into a fire is found intact in the embers and a miracle is declared.
1346	The convent of Begijnhof is founded.
1452	New laws forbid the use of thatch and timber in favour of brick and tile after a devastating fire.
1519	Charles V of Spain inherits Amsterdam with the Habsburg Empire.
1535	Anabaptists riot in Amsterdam, sparking a Catholic backlash.
1566	Calvinists storm churches, winning the right to hold public services – an event known as the *Beeldenstorm*, the Iconoclasm.
1567	Philip II of Spain, heir to Charles V, imposes strict Catholic rule.
1572	The Dutch revolt against Spanish rule.
1578	Prince William's troops drive the Spanish from Amsterdam. Catholicism is outlawed and Calvinists take over city institutions, an event known as the *Alteratie*, the Alteration.
1579	The northern Dutch provinces declare their independence from Spain. Protestants from Antwerp come to Amsterdam, heralding the Golden Age.
1595–7	The Dutch discover sea routes to Indonesia.
1602	Dutch East India Company set up to co-ordinate Dutch Far East trade.
1613	Construction of the canal circle begins.
1621	The Dutch West India Company is set up to co-ordinate trade with the Americas and Africa.
1689	The Dutch prince, William III of Orange, is crowned King of England.

18th century	Amsterdam's maritime trade is slowly crippled by a series of costly wars.		**1928**	Olympic Games hosted.
1795	The Velvet Revolution; French revolutionary troops are welcomed to Amsterdam by reformers who establish a new National Assembly.		**1945**	Amsterdam liberated from German occupation.
			1963	Squatter protests against the housing problem.
1806	Napoleon sets his brother, Louis Napoleon, on the Dutch throne.		**1965**	Anarchistic 'Provocateurs' win seats on Amsterdam's city council.
1813	The northern and southern provinces of The Netherlands are briefly united.		**1975**	Riots over plans to demolish an area of Nieuwmarkt to build the Metro system and Stadhuis complex.
1831	The southern provinces form the Kingdom of Belgium.		**1982**	Three days of rioting following the forcible eviction of squatters.
1845	Riots lead to democratic reform and a directly elected parliament under JR Thorbecke.		**1994**	Local council elections swing to the right.
1848–76	The Noordzee Kanaal (North Sea Canal) and the discovery of new diamond fields in South Africa spells prosperity for Amsterdam.		**1995**	Increasing drug problems lead to a closing down of coffee shops selling drugs.
			2002	The Netherlands adopts the euro. National election following the assassination of LPF party leader Pim Fortuyn. The right-wing CDA-LPF coalition wins.
1914–18	Though neutral, the city suffers the effects of anti-German food blockades.		**2005**	Dutch voters reject a proposed European Union constitution.

Governance

The Netherlands has a three-tier system of government: the national parliament based in Den Haag (The Hague) is responsible for defence, overall fiscal policy and foreign affairs; provincial councils based in each of the 12 provincial capitals are responsible for managing the local infrastructure; and city councils are responsible for running the large municipalities.

Amsterdam's World Trade Centre

The system is highly devolved and the Amsterdam city council has a very wide range of powers and responsibilities, while national politics has very little impact on the city. In recent years the council has had to face an awesome range of issues, and it has developed progressive, though not always successful, policies to manage the problems of housing, unemployment, race relations, inner-city renewal, drugs and crime.

In the 1970s, what had hitherto been a series of relatively peaceful protests turned violent. On 'Blue Monday', 24 March 1975, police and protesters battled in the streets over plans to demolish an area of Nieuwmarkt to build the new Stadhuis or City Hall. In 1982, a state of emergency was declared after attempts by the police to evict squatters sparked off three days of rioting. Amsterdam was seen as one of the most troubled cities in Europe.

Today the anarchy of previous decades has given way to hard-headed pragmatism, tempered by traditional Dutch humanism. Local residents and shop owners have begun to form action groups to clean up their areas of the city and to apply pressure on the city council to tackle the problems of housing, drugs and petty crime.

Various experiments have been tried to tackle the drugs problem. Initially, non-Dutch addicts were deported and the remainder were given free heroin in an attempt to stamp out illegal dealing and petty crime. This proved unsuccessful and the authorities have now placed their hopes in a programme of medical help for heroin addicts, whose numbers have now stabilised.

On the housing front, the squatter movement had one lasting effect: the wholesale clearance of 'slum' areas has been halted in favour of sympathetic small-scale regeneration. The city owns 40 per cent of the housing stock and 70 per cent of the land; its policy now is to lease this to developers who build new apartments or restore old buildings for rent. Critics say that rents have soared as a result, and there are long waiting lists for attractive canal-side flats.

On the other hand, problems remain beyond the city centre. Amsterdam has a large ethnic community; nearly a third of the city's 735,000 population are of Turkish or Moroccan origin. Many were brought in as 'guest workers' in the 1960s; others originate from former Dutch colonies – the Antilles, Surinam and Indonesia. Many live in soulless tower blocks on estates such as Bijlmermeer, in the south of the city. Ironically, these flats, designed on the futuristic principles of Le Corbusier, were originally built as luxury apartments, but their intended occupants preferred to stay in the city centre.

Part of the answer has been to redevelop Bijlmermeer, replacing the tower blocks with new housing on a more human scale. Businesses have been encouraged to open up here as well as to provide the much-needed local employment.

Amsterdam's problems have been made worse by the closure of several big industrial enterprises, such as the former shipyards. Other businesses have moved, many to Rotterdam. Heineken's decision to relocate to Zoeterwoude in 1986 was a further blow, even though residents had often complained about the smell of the brewery and its massive trucks clogging up the city's narrow roads.

In response to the threat of decline and unemployment, a huge regeneration scheme is under way in the redundant docklands area which stretches for 15km behind Amsterdam Centraal Station. It is hoped that multinational companies will be attracted to set up corporate headquarters here from which to take advantage of the single European market.

In a complex city like Amsterdam it is difficult to find political solutions that please everyone, yet much has been achieved since the stormy days of the 1970s. Slowly but surely the city council is achieving its objective of *stadsvernieuwing* – urban renewal (the Zeedijk area, on the fringe of the red-light district, being the latest to benefit); instead of ending up a ghost town or a gigantic tourist theme park, Amsterdam remains an invigorating, cultural and energetic city that Amsterdammers genuinely like to live in.

The Houses of Parliament, seat of the Dutch government

Culture

Amsterdam has its own distinctive culture which embraces the extremes of tradition and the avant-garde. On the one hand, Amsterdammers are wedded to the old-world charm of brown cafés lit by *schemerlampen*, twilight lamps that cast a golden glow. Crowds gather around streetside herring stalls in spring to sample the mild *nieuwe haring*, the first of the season, while all over the city bright ornate barrel organs pump out old-fashioned fairground music.

Amusement cart on a Kalverstraat street

On the other hand, this is a city that loves the experimental. Theatres mount próductions in which the cast consists entirely of barking Alsatian dogs. Galleries host 'events' where participants transform each other into living works of art by daubing their naked bodies with paint. Amsterdam could never be accused of dreariness.

Such contradictions are part of the cultural diversity of a city which sometimes seems obsessed by art – not surprising when you consider how many Amsterdammers make their living in architecture, design, photography, journalism and other creative professions. Sometimes passions run out of control. The *Night Watch* has been attacked with knives and acid on several occasions by frustrated individuals, envious that their own work does not attract as much attention as Rembrandt's masterpiece.

Such extreme gestures are hardly justified in a city that offers so many outlets for creative expression. Artists receive training grants and subsidies, and both public and commercial money is used to fund public murals, paintings or sculpture whenever a new building is erected in the city. The city's streets are awash with performers: Dam Square, Leidseplein, Stationsplein and Vondelpark throng with buskers in summer, and punk rockers, acrobats and puppeteers compete for attention with bongo players and mime artists. Some of the city's buses and trams have been turned into mobile works of art by students of the Rietveld Academy. Even shopkeepers and homeowners enter into the spirit of artistic endeavour; the shopping streets of Jordaan and the canal circle are enlivened by eye-catching window displays and the owners of smart canalside apartments leave their curtains open at night to reveal tasteful interiors – every item of furniture, every plant and picture carefully chosen to make a statement to any passer-by.

Several times a year Amsterdammers come together for big street festivals; for Queen's Day, Koninginnedag (30 April), for carnival, for the Aalsmeer to Amsterdam floral parade in the beginning of September and for the

Jordaan festival in the middle of the month. Here again Amsterdam reveals its love of extremes. Traditional accordion players and oompah bands alternate with heavy rock and experimental jazz bands to entertain the crowds on makeshift stages set up in front of street cafés. Everyone wears fancy dress, ranging from the freakish to the chic. All heads turn at the arrival of a popular character, known simply as Fabiola, whose outlandish and inventive costumes have now become part of Amsterdam folklore. Further style is added by the ethnic costumes worn by the large number of Caribbean, Surinamese and Indonesian participants.

Two further set-piece events attract festive crowds. In June some of the world's top performers come together for the three week-long Holland Festival. On the last weekend in August, theatre, dance and music companies from all over The Netherlands perform extracts from the year's forthcoming programme in the streets of Amsterdam. This event, called the *Uitmarkt*, is a huge open-air arts market designed to sell advance tickets; for the visitor it provides an opportunity to sample the complete spectrum of the arts, from the conventional to the way-out fringe. Other events to look out for in the summer are the cheap and varying summer concerts in July and August in the famous Concertgebouw and the Grachten festival on Herengracht, Keizersgracht and Prinsengracht around the third Saturday of August. During the rest of the year the cultural calendar is packed with events: opera and ballet at the Muziektheater, concerts by the world-renowned Royal Concertgebouw Orchestra (under Mariss Jansons) or The Netherlands Philharmonic Orchestra, jazz at the Bimhuis, world music at the Melkweg (Milky Way), and rock concerts at Paradiso, not to mention scores of events hosted by small clubs and arts cafés. Amsterdam is famed for its tolerance, its live-and-let-live philosophy, and in that atmosphere, cultural pluralism thrives – there is no taste, no matter how traditional or way out, that is not catered for.

Enjoying the warm glow of a *bruine kroegen* (brown café)

Festivals

The people of Amsterdam are always ready to take to the streets and join in the spontaneous fun that surrounds their numerous festivals. Visitors are welcome to join in and flow with the crowd.

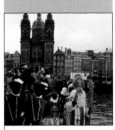

St Nicolaas Feast

January
New Year is greeted with fireworks and firecrackers, a symbolic way of scaring off the devils and ghosts of dreary winter. Revellers sustain themselves by consuming quantities of *oliebollen* (doughnuts) and champagne. The big squares, such as Nieuwmarkt, Leidseplein, Rembrandtplein and Dam Square, see most of the action, and street performers of every kind take their turn at entertaining the crowds.

February/March
If the weather turns cold enough to freeze the canals and waterways, an event that occurs only once in every ten years or so, everyone brings out their skates. In the northern Netherlands, the big event, weather permitting, is the **Elfstedentocht**, the 11-towns race, a real test of skaters' skill and stamina, which Amsterdammers keenly follow on television.

April
30 April is **Koninginnedag** (Queen's Day), the Queen's official birthday (her real birthday is on 31 January). Once this was a festival for children, who would set up stalls selling their handmade sweets and cakes or unwanted toys, to earn some pocket money, but today everyone joins in, setting up stalls in front of their homes so that Amsterdam turns into a huge street market. Buskers and street performers add to the fun and many bars set up outdoor stages where jazz, folk and rock bands entertain the customers. Leidseplein and Vondelpark are the best places to savour the atmosphere.

May
After the **Commemoration of 4 May** for the victims of World War II, the end of the German occupation is celebrated on the 5th as **Liberation Day**, with concerts, parties and historical processions.

June
The three-week long **Holland Festival** is a prestigious showcase for the arts – dance, ballet, theatre, music and opera. Top performers from all over the world take part (programme information from Holland Festival, *www.hollandfestival.nl. Tel: (020) 530 7110*).

July
The **Over Het IJ Festival** is in full swing, with fringe-style arts events all over the part of Amsterdam that few visitors

penetrate – the north bank of the IJ river, reached by a (free) passenger ferry that shuttles back and forth from behind Centraal Station. Performances take place indoors and out, and range across the whole spectrum of progressive arts, from dance to electronic sound and light shows (*tel: (020) 624 6380* for information and bookings).

August

One of the most enjoyable events of the year takes place from the second Wednesday to the second Saturday: **The Grachtenfestival** provides free classical music on and around Prinsengracht, culminating in the concert on Saturday evening. This usually features a top international pianist who performs from a floating platform in front of the Pulitzer Hotel (Prinsengracht 315–331). Music-lovers come with picnics and champagne to line the canal banks (for information *tel: (020) 421 4542*).

At the end of the month, the Museum Quarter hosts the **Uitmarkt**, a huge cultural fair at which arts companies from all over The Netherlands perform extracts from their forthcoming season's programme in order to help ticket sales.

September

The **Bloemen Corso** (Flower Parade), held on the first Saturday in September, is a spectacular affair organised by florists and horticulturalists; their huge and decorative floats, smothered in flowers, are driven from the flower auction at Aalsmeer through the streets of Amsterdam to a reception in Dam Square, after which the parade is illuminated for the return to Aalsmeer.

Open Monument Days (National), on the second weekend in September, provides an opportunity to see inside some of Amsterdam's finest protected monuments and buildings, including private homes and office premises in the canal circle.

The **Jordaan Festival**, in the third weekend of September, is a riotous fortnight of music, fancy dress and beer-drinking in which the Jordaan district extends a friendly welcome to all comers.

November/December

St Nicolaas, the Dutch equivalent of Santa Claus, arrives in Amsterdam on the second or third Saturday in November (around the 17th), arriving by steamboat 'from Spain' at Centraal Station and parading up Damrak, distributing sweets to crowds of children. Dutch children traditionally receive their presents on the **Feast of St Nicolaas** (5 December), although increasingly they are indulged with a second round of presents on 25 December as well.

Singing in celebration of Queen's Day

First Steps

The historic heart of Amsterdam is very compact and it can be crossed on foot in less than half an hour. Trams which depart from Amsterdam Centraal Station reach all parts of the city, and a Museumboat service circles the canal system every 30 minutes in summer from 9.30am–4.45pm. (For further details, *see* Public Transport *in the* Practical Guide.)

A canal cruise is a must for visitors

Even so, the best way to get to know the city is to walk. If you take to the streets in comfortable shoes, you will be rewarded by glimpses of Amsterdam at work and play and discover the rich diversity of the city's architecture. Enticing shops selling flowers, crafts, antiques or books will arrest your attention and when you are tired you can be sure there is a pavement café, serving coffee or *warme chocolade* (hot chocolate) topped with whipped cream, waiting just round the corner.

Another way to gain a swift overview of the city is to take a canal cruise; knowledgeable guides will point out the key buildings and features and, seen from the water as it was intended to be, Amsterdam takes on a whole new perspective.

AREA BY AREA

When viewed on a map, Amsterdam has a distinctive shape; its several districts lock together like pieces in a jigsaw, and they represent separate phases in the deliberately planned development of the city. Once you understand the city's layout you will find it easier to negotiate the cobweb-like pattern of canals, streets and squares.

The Medieval City

Nearly everyone receives their first glimpse of Amsterdam from Centraal Station, the arrival point of trains from the airport and from all over Europe. The station stands on the site of the original harbour which was partly filled in during the 19th century. From Stationsplein, which is usually crowded with buskers and commuters, the city's main street – Damrak – leads to the main square. This is simply called Dam Square and, as the name suggests, it is built over the site of the original dam across the River Amstel, after which the city was named. This dam probably had lock gates, allowing small craft to pass through, and was designed to control the tidal flow of the river. Two of the city's most imposing buildings stand on the right-hand (western) side of the square: the Koninklijk Paleis (Royal Palace) and the Nieuwe Kerk (New Church).

Damrak runs through the heart of the oldest part of Amsterdam, dividing it into two parts which, on the map, look like a pair of lungs. To the east (left, with your back to the station) is the Oude Zijde (OZ), or Old Side, district, which was already built up by the 13th century. To the west is the slightly younger Nieuwe Zijde (NZ), or New Side, district, first developed in the 14th century.

Medieval Amsterdam was surrounded by a defensive rampart. This has since disappeared, but its position is indicated by the names of Oudezijds Voorburgwal and Oudezijds Achterburgwal meaning, respectively, in front of and behind the city wall. These two canals themselves started out as defensive moats. Their

counterparts to the west, the Nieuwezijds Voorburgwal and Achterburgwal, have since been filled in.

The Canal Circle

Wrapped around the core of the medieval city is the Grachtengordel, the Canal Circle, consisting of three concentric canals built in the 17th century and the main focus of architectural interest in the city. The harbour end of the Canal Circle, around Brouwersgracht, was the first to be developed, beginning in 1613. As building progressed the houses became ever grander; the point in the canal furthest from the harbour is known as the Golden Bend because

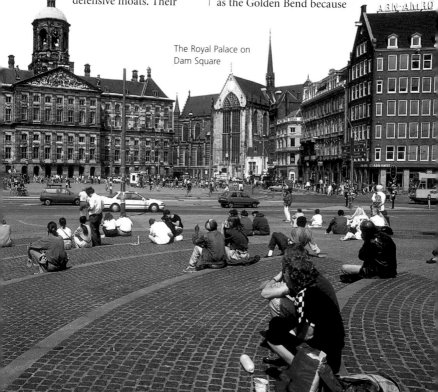

The Royal Palace on Dam Square

Central Amsterdam

of the wealth of its former inhabitants and the palatial splendour of their houses, many of which now serve as bank premises and embassies.

The Museum Quarter

Not far from the Golden Bend is the Museum Kwartier (Museum Quarter), a wedge-shaped block built as an extension to the city in the 19th century. Here you will find the famous Rijksmuseum and Van Gogh Museum, as well as the Stedelijk Museum of

Rijksmuseum – one of Amsterdam's major highlights

Modern Art. Bordering the Museum Quarter are Vondelpark, the scene of open-air concerts in summer, and the Concertgebouw, famed for its orchestra and excellent acoustics.

A short way further out is the district called De Pijp (The Pipe), because of its long, narrow tunnel-like streets. The principal thoroughfare, Albert Cuypstraat, hosts a bustling and colourful street market where it is possible to buy just about anything. The street is also renowned for its inexpensive ethnic restaurants and the Van Moppes Diamonds factory.

The Museum Quarter is linked to the city centre by Nieuwe Spiegelstraat, which ends close to the Golden Bend. It has the biggest concentration of antique shops in Amsterdam and makes for

fascinating browsing. The canal circle continues round from here until it is interrupted by the River Amstel. It then continues for a short way on the opposite bank to meet the district

Greater Amsterdam

The Van Gogh Museum

known as Plantage. As the name suggests, this is a leafy suburb which was originally laid out as a pleasure garden; by the late 18th century wealthy businessmen began to build country houses here, but several large green spaces remain, such as the zoo (known as Natura Artis Magistra, or just Artis) and the Hortus Botanicus Plantage (Botanical Gardens).

The Magerebrug or `Skinny Bridge'

The Jewish Quarter

Coming back towards the city centre, the next district is Jodenbuurt, the former Jewish Quarter, with its synagogues, the Jewish Historical Museum and the Museum Het Rembrandthuis (Rembrandt's House). Jodenbuurt has been comprehensively redeveloped since World War II and has a character entirely different to the rest of central Amsterdam, dominated as it is by the controversial new Stadhuis (City Hall) and the Muziektheater complex, home to the Netherlands Opera and National Ballet.

The familiar Amsterdam of characterful canals and old houses returns as you cross from Jodenbuurt into Nieuwmarkt, a district of great contrasts. To the south is the attractive maze of buildings forming the university, while to the north, around Zeedijk, are the red-light district and Chinatown.

Amsterdam has several other districts of note. The eastern harbour, adjacent to Plantage and Jodenbuurt, has numerous old warehouses recently converted to apartments, and the excellent Nederlands Scheepvaartmuseum (Dutch Maritime Museum). On the other side of the city, Jordaan (from the French *jardin*, garden) was, despite its name, an industrial suburb of narrow lanes and cramped workshops. Today it is a characterful neighbourhood of craft and speciality shops and ethnic restaurants.

The Character of Amsterdam

Amsterdam is an overgrown village, a comfortable congenial city whose relaxed pace is symbolised by the lumbering old-fashioned bicycles adopted by many residents for getting about, or the barges that make their sedate progress along the city's numerous canals.

At the same time, there are aspects to the city that may puzzle or shock the first-time visitor. Ugly graffiti disfigures many fine buildings and some streets are slippery with dog faeces. Dishevelled drug addicts loiter around the station, 'smoking bars' openly serve marijuana-laced cigarettes or cakes, and prostitutes operate in full public view from sitting rooms lit by red neon.

This side of Amsterdam reflects the city's live-and-let-live attitude, a philosophical outlook whose pluses and

Prostitutes overtly plying their trade

The Jewish Museum is devoted to the history of Amsterdam's Jewish population

minuses are a frequent topic of debate among Amsterdammers themselves. Fundamentally, Amsterdammers value freedom from interference – whether from neighbours or officialdom. In their respect for privacy they turn a blind eye to what others choose to do, even to the anti-social behaviour of dog owners and rebellious adolescents with spray cans.

As a result, Amsterdam has a tolerant, permissive culture, but one that has been exploited by the unscrupulous few,

BICYCLES

The bicycle is Amsterdam's favourite mode of transport – there are 550,000 bikes in a city of 735,000 people, many of them painted with colourful designs and transformed into minor works of art. The White Bikes scheme of 1966 was intended to provide free cycles for everyone; the scheme foundered in days when all the bikes were stolen, repainted and sold.

PLACE NAMES

To find your way about Amsterdam it helps to know that *plein* means square, *straat* street, *kerk* church, *huis* house and *gracht* canal. The three main canals are Herengracht (the Gentlemen's Canal), Keizersgracht (the Emperor's Canal, named after the Holy Roman Emperor, Maximilian I), and Prinsengracht (Prince's Canal, named after Prince William of Orange who liberated the city from Spanish rule).

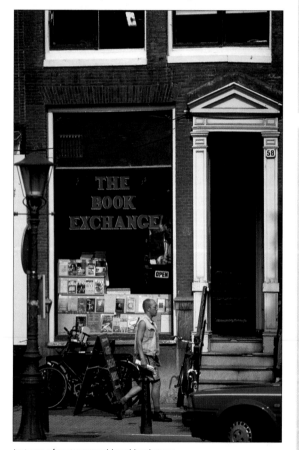

Just one of many second-hand bookstores

Lido Casino on Singelgracht

including the many drug dealers and pornographers who have tarnished the city's image. Though the municipality takes action against impudent behaviour, this still casts a shadow over what local people consider real achievements, such as racial harmony, the espousal of gay rights and sexual equality.

Amsterdammers will talk about such issues with humour and frankness; one of the delights of the city is the ease with which people engage in conversation, even with total strangers. They have the linguistic skills to do so; 70 per cent of the city's population speaks English and many also speak French and German. The Dutch educational system encourages language learning from an early age and Amsterdammers remain linguistically adroit by watching or listening to European TV and radio; many prefer the output of the British BBC to that of their own rather stolid national broadcasting authority.

They also read voraciously – Amsterdam is one of Europe's largest markets for books, and shelves full of well-thumbed volumes in several languages are an essential part of the furnishings in any self-respecting city home. Central to all this is one overriding characteristic: respect for the quality of life. Amsterdammers are entrepreneurial but not workaholic; furthering their careers is less important than family life, time spent with friends, or a visit to the theatre. Many visitors find that this refreshing and admirable attitude is highly infectious.

What to See

'*Where else in the world could one choose a place where all life's commodities and all the curiosities one could wish for are so easy to find as here?*'

RENÉ DESCARTES

Archaeological displays at
Allard Pierson Museum

Agnietenkapel

The Agnietenkapel is a simple but graceful chapel dating from 1470 and once part of the convent of St Agnes. In 1632 it was taken over by the Atheneum Illustre, a learned body out of which the University of Amsterdam was later to evolve. Part of the chapel was converted into a lecture theatre, the Grote Gehoorzaal, which has a fine wooden ceiling decorated with Renaissance motifs and a portrait of Minerva, goddess of wisdom. The walls of the theatre are hung with 17th-century portraits of illustrious and learned figures of the age. The rest of the building houses the Universiteitsmuseum (University Museum), a collection covering the history of education and student life in the city.

Oudezijds Voorburgwal 231. Tel: (020) 525 3339. The chapel is being renovated and will re-open in 2007. Trams: 4, 9, 14, 16, 24 or 25. Nearby: Allard Pierson Museum.

Allard Pierson Museum

This little-visited museum houses the University of Amsterdam's rich collection of archaeological material – mainly from ancient Egypt, Greece, Rome, Tuscany and the Near East.

It also displays plaster casts of ancient Greek and Roman sculpture and occasionally mounts excellent special exhibitions on specific themes.

Oude Turfmarkt 127. Tel: (020) 525 2556; www.uba.uva.nl/apm Open: Tue–Fri 10am–5pm, weekends & public holidays 1–5pm. Closed: Mon, 1 Jan, Easter Sunday, 30 Apr, Whit Sunday, 25 & 31 Dec. Admission charge. Trams: 4, 9, 16, 24 or 25. Nearby: Agnietenkapel, the University Quarter (see pp96–7).

Amstelkring Museum

The Amstelkring Museum is also known as *Ons Lieve Heer op Solder* (Our Lord in the Attic) because, concealed in the roof space of this group of three houses, there is a clandestine Catholic church. The delightful museum thus provides two quite different experiences. At one level, this is a fine example of a wealthy merchant's residence, built by Jan Hartman in 1661, complete with contemporary furnishings. But one sober-looking cupboard opens up to reveal bawdy, low-life scenes painted on the insides of the door! Upstairs is a splendid Baroque church with ingenious foldaway pulpit and altar, and hiding places for the priest and communion plate. Clandestine churches such as this date from the *Alteratie*, the Alteration of

1578. Until then Amsterdam was a Catholic city, but tolerant of Protestants and free-thinkers, refugees from persecution in other parts of Europe. Calvinists formed a large and influential group, but they were forbidden from holding public services until they rioted in 1566, breaking into the city's churches and smashing statues, an event known as the *Beeldenstorm*, the Iconoclasm.

Order was restored when Calvinists were given their own church in the city, but this in turn provoked a reaction from Philip II of Spain, Holy Roman Emperor and staunch defender of the Catholic faith. He sent 10,000 troops under the Duke of Alva, Fernando Alvarez de Toledo, to restore strict Catholic order in The Netherlands. Many Calvinists in Amsterdam were executed and others fled to England.

The Dutch revolt against Spanish repression began in 1572 under the leadership of William the Silent, Prince of Orange, whose volunteer army slowly drove the Spanish southwards, to the area of modern Belgium. They liberated Amsterdam in 1578, the year of the *Alteratie*, so-called because Protestants took over all the city's institutions and Catholicism, from then onwards, was banned – hence the growth of secret churches, of which the Amstelkring Museum has the best-preserved example.

In 1661, when this church was built, Catholics still went to great lengths to conceal their worship. By 1740, when the church was remodelled and given its galleries, capable of seating 200 people, it could scarcely still be operating without the knowledge of the authorities, who must simply have turned a blind eye. The ban on Catholicism was finally lifted in the 19th century when the nearby church of Sint Nicolaas was built, now standing forlorn and rarely used on the harbour, opposite Amsterdam Centraal Station.

Oudezijds Voorburgwal 40. Tel: (020) 624 6604; www.museumamstelkring.nl Open: Mon–Sat 10am–5pm, Sun & public holidays 1–5pm. Closed: 1 Jan & 30 Apr. Admission charge. Trams: 4, 9, 16, 24 & 25. Nearby: Oude Kerk (see pp46–7).

The fascinating Amstelkring Museum

Amsterdam's remarkable Grachtengordel, or Canal Ring, represents one of the earliest examples of deliberate town planning in Europe. The scheme was devised by Hendrik Staets, the municipal carpenter, in 1609. His plan for the controlled expansion of the city has an elegant logic. Three new canals were dug, the Herengracht, Keizersgracht and Prinsengracht, with a combined length of 12km. Each canal is 25m wide, broad enough to accommodate four lanes of barges or lighters, the small, shallow-draughted boats used to unload cargo from bigger ships moored in the harbour. Up to 4,000 boats could be accommodated and 17th-century engravings show the canal circle as a forest of masts, its wide, tree-shaded quays bustling with porters.

Housing plots were sold to merchants with precisely 30m of frontage, though some variation can be detected among the general uniformity; sometimes property speculators bought up two adjoining plots and resold them as one, enabling palatial residences to be built, or they subdivided them into three narrower plots.

Planning laws stipulated the maximum depth of houses to ensure a degree of space and light between houses backing on to each other on adjacent canals. This garden space was, in some cases, built over at a later date to provide an *achterhuis*, a back annexe, such as the one in which Anne Frank and her family hid from Nazi persecution. Even so, the canal circle still has numerous hidden gardens, as anyone who climbs the tower of Westerkerk will discover.

Shops were only permitted on the narrow interlinking radial canals, which is where they are still found to this day. This policy ensured that the three principal canals present an unbroken vista of houses, individualised by ornate gables and cornices, sculptural reliefs and fine doorcases; spotting the endless variations is one of the great pleasures of a leisurely stroll round this most elegant of cities.

Facing page: The view from the Oude Kerk, showing variations on a theme of pantiles and Flemish roofs
Above and right: Though there have been some modern and inelegant encroachments, the roofscape of Amsterdam remains remarkably intact and unspoiled

Walk: Central Amsterdam

This walk covers the main sights of the city centre and is intended to help you gain your bearings.
Allow 1 hour.

Start at Amsterdam Centraal Station.

1 Amsterdam Centraal

Amsterdam's palatial railway station was built in 1889 by PJH Cuypers, the same architect who designed the Rijksmuseum. Around 100,000 travellers pass through it every day but few stop to look at the magnificent sculptures depicting trade and industry. In its time the station was so admired that the Japanese built Tokyo station in the same style. The tower on the right displays a clock; its partner on the left has a wind-direction indicator.
With your back to the station look over to the left.

2 VVV Informatiekantoor (Tourist Information)

The city's main tourist information office is a useful reference point. It is located on the upper floor of a pretty timber building; below is the Noord-Zuid Hollandsch Koffiehuis (Coffee House), a popular spot for cakes and coffee.
Walk across Stationsplein and up Damrak.

3 Damrak

On the left, little more than a duck pond is all that remains of Amsterdam's original harbour, cut off from the sea when the station was built. Further up, the Beurs van Berlage stands on the site of the original Amsterdam Exchange.

It was rebuilt in late 19th-century style from 1896 to 1903 by HP Berlage and recently converted for use as a cultural centre. Next comes De Bijenkorf (The Beehive), which has the distinction of being the city's biggest department store.
Continue up Damrak to Dam Square.

4 Dam Square
To the right of the city's main square is the former Stadhuis (Town Hall), completed in 1655, and renamed the Koninklijk Paleis (Royal Palace) when Louis Napoleon took up residence in 1808. It is partnered by the tall Gothic Nieuwe Kerk (New Church) which was begun in 1408.

To the left is the Nationaal Monument commemorating the dead of World War II. The 22-m high obelisk contains urns of earth from each Dutch province and from Indonesia. Naked chained figures represent war victims and the inscription reads 'Never again'.
Cross the square to the right of the Peek & Cloppenburg department store and enter Kalverstraat, the city's main shopping street, all brash neon and blaring music. Halfway down, beyond Marks & Spencer, look for a lop-sided gateway dated 1581.

5 Amsterdams Historisch Museum
The gate, with its figures of uniformed children, leads to the former municipal orphanage, now the Historical Museum. Walk into the arcaded courtyard and left, through glass doors, into the Civic Guard Gallery; this corridor is lined with 17th-century portraits of the city's militia units.

At the opposite end of the gallery, exit through the doors, turn right and, keeping to the left, descend two steps into the Begijnhof.

6 Begijnhof
This peaceful former convent is now a home for *ongehuwde dames* (unmarried ladies). Follow the path round to the Engelsekerk (English Church), built in 1607. Opposite is Het Houten Huis (The Wooden House), built in 1460 and the oldest surviving building in Amsterdam.
Alongside is a passage leading out on to Spui. Turn right and cross to the paved area in front of the Athenaeum Bookshop.

7 Het Amsterdamse Lieverdje
The name of this bronze statue means 'The Lovable Rascal of Amsterdam' and it is surrounded by bookshops and popular pavement cafés.
Retrace your steps past the Begijnhof entrance and walk down Rozenboomsteeg, past the elegant Empire-style building that houses Esprit. Turn right in Kalverstraat and continue all the way to the Munttoren.

8 Munttoren
This grey stone tower was once a gate in the medieval city wall. The carillon of bells plays every 15 minutes. The tower was briefly used in 1672–3 for minting coins, hence its name. The walk ends just across the bridge to the right of the tower – at the Bloemenmarkt, where traders sell flowers and plants from floating barges.
To return to Dam Square, simply retrace your steps down Kalverstraat.

Amsterdams Historisch Museum

The Amsterdam Historical Museum is a must for those who want to understand the history and development of the city. It is located just off Kalverstraat, the city's main shopping thoroughfare. The entrance is easy to miss amidst all the brash neon – just a narrow leaning gateway decorated with the imperial crown and triple cross of Amsterdam's coat of arms. Below, a sculptural relief of children dressed in blue and red uniforms reminds us that the museum occupies the buildings of the former municipal orphanage, founded in 1580 on the site of St Lucien's convent. When you pass through the arch, the museum café is on the right, occupying the former convent dairy. It serves excellent pancakes and is known as 'David and Goliath Café' after the huge wooden fairground figures of David and Goliath standing at one end.

Beyond lies a series of beautifully restored buildings designed by two leading 17th-century architects, Hendrik de Keyser and Jacob van Campen. They surround quiet cobbled courtyards where the orphanage children used to play. The prestige of the buildings is an indication of the city's enlightened policy in providing for the care of the poor – long before the idea of a welfare state was conceived.

It is a good idea to start your visit to the museum in room 1 (on the ground floor) where a computer animation shows you how Amsterdam grew from a tiny 13th-century fishing community to the modern city it is today.

The next two rooms (2 and 3) contain archaeological finds, reconstructed rooms and contemporary paintings illustrating life and industry in the medieval city. A part of room 3, for instance, is devoted to the Miracle of Amsterdam which occurred in 1345. The rather unsavoury details concern a dying man who was given communion as part of the Last Rites but who vomited up the host; this was thrown on a fire but found intact in the embers the next day. A miracle was declared and Amsterdam became a pilgrimage centre, so important that even the Holy Roman Emperor, Maximilian I, came to be cured of an illness. The Miracle is still celebrated today by up to 10,000 Catholics who take part in the *Stille Omgang* – the Silent Procession – which passes through the city's streets the second Sunday in March.

Room 4 houses the famous woodcut of 1544 by Cornelis Athonieszoon, showing a three-dimensional bird's-eye view of the city and its bustling harbour.

The Golden Age relived in the Historical Museum

Clearly visible on this map is the original dam across the Amstel and its associated sea dyke walls.

Rooms 4 to 7 illustrate aspects of the city in the 16th century and especially the Golden Age (17th century). Another illuminated map shows the main Dutch voyages of discovery that set out from Amsterdam from 1595 looking first for a northeastern passage to the East Indies, then blazing a trail round the Cape of Good Hope. Typical eastern imports are displayed – blue-and-white Chinese porcelain that gave rise to the Dutch Delftware industry, sugar, tea and spices. A colourful contemporary painting shows Dam square at that time, crowded with beggars, street musicians, artists selling their products, prosperous burghers in their finery – in fact little different from today, except for the changes in dress!

Rooms 8 to 11 (on the first floor) look at the art and crafts of the 17th century and a small loft above Room 10 is devoted to carillon music, a distinctive feature of the city's churches; here you can sit at a keyboard and play tunes on bells suspended above.

Before you go to room 11 you could visit the Civic Guard Gallery, a glassed-in public thoroughfare hung with militia company portraits. Room 11 itself contains more group portraits – of the regents who supervised the city's charitable institutions – and some big pictures of happy orphanage life. Room 12 gives an insight into bourgeois life in 18th-century Amsterdam, all ponderous furniture and silverware, before livening up again with a brief account of industry. The museum

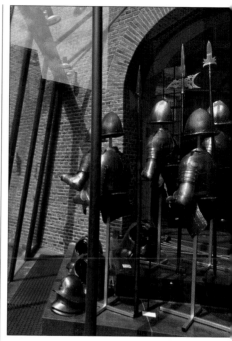

Arms and armour on display

concludes (in rooms 13 to 21 on the first floor and rooms 22 to 24 on the second floor) with the recent history of Amsterdam, from 1815 to the present. A pick of topics: social relations in the 19th century; the turn of the century; World War II; the Sixties, stamped by the anti-establishment Provo movement; gay rights; being young in Amsterdam. *Entrances at Kalverstraat 92, Nieuwezijds Voorburgwal 357 & Sint Luciensteeg 27. Tel: (020) 523 1822; www.ahm.nl Open: weekdays 10am–5pm, weekends & public holidays 11am–5pm. Closed: 1 Jan, 30 Apr & 25 Dec. Admission charge. Trams: 1, 2, 4, 5, 9, 16, 24 & 25. Nearby: Begijnhof (see p38).*

Anne Frank Huis

The Anne Frank House attracts more then half a million visitors a year and in summer it is essential to go early in the day to avoid long queues and crowded rooms. The house is tucked away on quiet Prinsengracht in the shadow of Westerkerk's tower, whose bells are lyrically described in Anne Frank's famous diary. It is a typical merchant's house, built in 1635, with an *achterhuis*, or back extension, added in 1740. In this attic the Frank family hid from July 1942 to August 1944.

The Franks had already escaped from Nazi persecution once in their lives; in 1933 they left their native Frankfurt, where Anne was born in 1929, and moved to Amsterdam, where they lived happily enough for seven years.

On 14 May 1940, the Nazis bombed Rotterdam: 800 people, mostly innocent civilians, were killed, 24,000 homes were destroyed and 50,000 people were left homeless. The Germans warned that they would next bomb Den Haag (The Hague), then Utrecht and all other Dutch cities in turn. Faced with such appalling aggression the Dutch had no choice but to surrender on 15 May: that night, knowing what was to come, 150 Jews in Amsterdam committed suicide.

Anti-Jewish measures began in earnest in 1940 with a series of prohibitive proclamations: Jews could not enter public places – swimming pools, parks and cinemas – or use public transport; all Jewish businesses had to be registered.

In February 1941, the Jewish Quarter of the city was closed off and the first of

Inside the haunting Anne Frank House

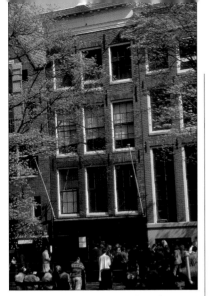

The back extension of this typical merchant's house hid the Frank family for two years

a series of round-ups, *razzias*, began. Thousands were arrested, herded into trains and sent off to Westerbork, a concentration camp on the Dutch–German border.

In 1942, Anne Frank's father, Otto, decided that the best course of action was to 'dive' – *onderduiken* – simply to disappear. He prepared a hiding place in the house that served as his company's office and warehouse. On 5 July a deportation order arrived, calling up Otto's eldest daughter, Margot, for 'work' at Westerbork. The next morning the family disappeared into the attic of Prinsengracht 263, their hiding place protected by nothing more solid than a bookcase concealing the stairs to the back of the house.

The Franks were joined by the van Daan family and a dentist, Albert Dussel. For two years this clandestine household survived with the help of Otto Frank's Dutch partners and his two office girls, Miep and Elli. Food was provided by a local greengrocer, one of several who played their part in the Resistance by supplying 'divers'.

Not everyone was so altruistic. Someone – never identified – betrayed the Franks to the Nazis in 1944. They were arrested and sent to Westerbork, by then a staging post for Bergen-Belsen, where Anne Frank died of hunger and disease in March 1945, aged 15. Of all the eight members of the secret household, only Otto Frank survived.

The Anne Frank House remains as it was in 1944, bare of furniture, which was looted after the family was deported. There are magazine pictures of film stars pasted on the wall by Anne and pencil marks recording the heights of the two growing sisters. The front of the building is used for exhibitions mounted by the Anne Frank Foundation, which is dedicated to combating prejudice, racism and discrimination in all its forms.

Anne Frank's diary, *Het Achterhuis* ('The Annexe'), was found lying on the floor after the family was arrested. It has since been published in 51 languages and vividly records the daily routine of life in the secret annexe, as well as the growing maturity of a naturally gifted writer, doomed to a tragic end.

One of the last entries in the diary states; 'I want to live on after my death'. That wish, at least, has been achieved. *Prinsengracht 263. Tel: (020) 556 7100; www.annefrank.nl Open: daily, Apr–Aug 9am–9pm, Sept–Mar 9am–7pm. Closed: Yom Kippur. Admission charge. Trams: 13, 14 & 17.* *Nearby: Westerkerk (see p47).*

Walk: Around Brouwersgracht

This walk covers the oldest part of the canal circle, the harbour end, which was laid out from 1613.
Allow 1½ hours.

Start at Amsterdam Centraal Station. The enormous weight of this structure proved so heavy for the pile foundations that it suffered partial subsidence during construction in 1885. Walk up Damrak and take the first alley on the right, Haringpakkerssteeg, then bear right in Nieuwendijk. Cross busy Martelaarsgracht, turn left up Spuistraat and take the first right, Kattengat.

1 Ronde Lutherse Kerk

The big building on the left, with its green copper dome, is the Lutheran Round Church, built in 1668, and now used as a conference centre and concert hall. Beside the church are two attractive step-gabled houses built in 1614 by Hendrik de Keyser – De Gouden Spiegel and De Silveren Spiegel (The Golden Mirror and The Silver Mirror).
Walk on past the Round Church, into Stromarkt (Straw Market), then left on to Singel.

2 Singel

Number 7, is the smallest house in Amsterdam, only a door's width wide. The owner may have built the house like this to avoid property taxes, which were levied according to the width of the façade. To the right is Haarlemmersluis

(Haarlem Lock); before the IJsselmeer was dammed and ceased to be tidal, this lock controlled the water level in the whole canal network.
Walk back up Singel, cross the bridge by the lock, turn left down the opposite bank of Singel and right into Brouwersgracht.

3 Brouwersgracht
The Brewers' Canal is one of the most photogenic in the city; the right bank is lined with attractively converted 17th-century warehouses while the canal itself is crossed by numerous bridges providing a link to the three canals of the Grachtengordel. A short way up on the right, in Herenmarkt, is West-Indisch Huis, the headquarters of the Dutch West India Company from 1623.
Continue along Brouwersgracht to the Prinsengracht junction and turn left up to Noorderkerk.

4 Noorderkerk (North Church)
This vast church was designed by Hendrik de Keyser and built in 1620 to serve the working-class district of Jordaan, which lies to the right. The square in front hosts the Boerenmarkt (Farmers' Market) on Saturdays, the Lapjesmarkt, a large flea market (mainly for clothes), on Mondays.
Cross the next bridge left and walk down the opposite bank of Prinsengracht.

5 Hofjes
Two *hofjes*, or almshouses, can be visited. Zon's Hofje (Nos 159–71; push the door open and walk down the corridor) is a tree-shaded courtyard dating from 1765. Van Brienenhofje (Nos 89–133) dates from 1804 – legend

has it that Jan van Brienen, a merchant, founded it after he was rescued from imminent suffocation, having locked himself inside his own safe.
Backtrack up Prinsengracht and turn left to explore Prinsenstraat and Herenstraat, then walk up Keizersgracht.

6 Het Huis met de Hoofden
The 'House with the Heads,' Keizersgracht 123, was built by Hendrik de Keyser in 1623 and is decorated with busts of Greek deities – Apollo, Ceres, Ares, Athene, Dionysus and Artemis.
Turn right on Leliegracht, a cross street noted for its bookshops and especially No. 22, Architectura et Natura, which specialises in books on architecture, wildlife and gardening. Turn left on Prinsengracht.

7 Anne Frank Huis
Prinsengracht 263 is where Anne Frank wrote her famous diary while hiding with her family from the Nazis between July 1942 and August 1944.
Continue a short way up to Westerkerk.

8 Westerkerk
The West Church (*see p47*) was built to Hendrik de Keyser's design in 1623 and its tower can be climbed for a bird's-eye view of the canal circle.
From Westerkerk, turn left and follow Raadhuisstraat to return to Dam Square.

Nearby
Walking down Raadhuisstraat, take a diversion to the left a short way into Herengracht for the ornate Bartolotti House (Nos 170–72), and the Theatermuseum next door (No. 168).

Begijnhof

The Begijnhof is a secluded oasis of peace in the bustling heart of the city. The entrance, easily missed, is a narrow door on Spui that leads into a flowery tree-shaded courtyard where neat gardens front some of Amsterdam's most charming houses. Number 34, known as the **Het Houten Huis** or Wooden House, is the oldest surviving in the city, dating back to around 1470.

The Begijnhof was founded in 1346 as a convent for Beguines, named after Lambert de Begué who founded the order in Liège in the 12th century. The order – popular in the Low Countries and Germany – enabled women to live in a convent, devoting themselves to charitable work, but without taking vows of poverty, obedience and chastity. They remained free to own property, leave the convent and marry.

After the *Alteratie* of 1578 (*see* Amstelkring Museum, *pp26–7*) when Catholic institutions were taken over by Protestants, the Beguines were allowed to continue their work of education, caring for the poor and nursing the sick. They could worship only in secret, however, and a clandestine chapel, the Begijnhofkapel, was built in 1671, hidden behind the domestic façade of No. 30. The chapel can be visited; its entrance is opposite the former convent church, handed over to Scottish Presbyterians in 1607 and subsequently renamed the Engelse Kerk, the English Church. This was rebuilt in 1727, and a more recent addition is the pulpit, with panels designed by Mondrian. As well as remaining the main church of Amsterdam's British community, the Engelse Kerk hosts a series of free lunchtime concerts in July and August and evening concerts during the rest of the year (details posted at the church door, or telephone *(020) 624 9665*).

Many of the buildings of the Begijnhof were 'modernised' by the addition of new façades in the 17th and 18th centuries. The last of the Beguines died in 1971 and the houses are now let, for a nominal rent, to elderly women and female students.

Entrance at Spui No. 14 or from the Amsterdam Historical Museum.
Open: daily 9am–5pm.
Begijnhofkapel open: most days 9am–6.30pm; www.begijnhofamsterdam.nl
Engelse Kerk open: only for concerts and for services on Sun at 10.30am. Free admission. Trams: 1, 2, 4, 5, 9, 16, 24 & 25. Nearby: Amsterdams Historich Museum (see pp32–3).

Bijbels Museum (Biblical Museum)

This specialised collection is devoted to the history of the Old and New Testaments and is an important research centre for Jewish and Christian scholars. The displays illustrate life in biblical times through archaeological material and reconstructions of key buildings, such as the Temple of Solomon. For many visitors the appeal is the house itself, with its stately period details and ceiling paintings by Jacob Wit.

The house is part of a row (Nos 362 to 328) designed in 1662 by Philip Vingboons, one of the leading architects of the Golden Age. The builder was Jacob Cromhout who lived at No. 366, hence its alternative name, the Cromhouthuisen.

Herengracht 366. Tel: (020) 624 2436;
www.bijbelsmuseum.nl Open: Mon–Sat
10am–5pm; Sun & public holidays
11am–5pm. Closed: 1 Jan & 30 Apr.
Admission charge. Trams: 1, 2 or 5.
Nearby: Begijnhof.

Beurs Van Berlage

Amsterdam's Beurs, the former Stock
Exchange, was reopened as a cultural
centre in 1988, and is worth visiting for
its interesting exhibitions and for
concerts given by The Netherlands
Philharmonic Orchestra who have their
home here, and as an architectural
spectacle in its own right. The Beurs was
rebuilt from 1896 to 1903 by Hendrick
Petrus Berlage, the best Dutch architect
of his age, in an imaginative style that
anticipates the work of the early 1900s'
Amsterdam School (*see p80*) and is
regarded as The Netherland's most
important 20th-century building. The
superb interiors are a tour de force of
patterned brickwork and colourful tiles
under a glass and wrought-iron roof.
The building is used for changing
exhibitions, and is only open during
these.
Damrak 277. Tel: (020) 530 4141
(general enquiries); (020) 521 7575
(box office); www.beursvanberlage.nl
Box office open: Tue–Fri 2–5pm, other
times for concerts. Trams: 4, 9, 16, 24 &
25. The Beurs is best seen by visiting an
exhibition or joining a guided
architectural tour. Nearby: Oude Kerk
(see pp46–7).

A glimpse of biblical times at the Biblical Museum

Canal Life

Canals give Amsterdam its distinctive character, but it is a mistake to call the city the 'Venice of the North'. Amsterdammers are proud that their city is a vital, living place – to them Venice is a dead city, a theme park abandoned to tourism.

Swans, ducks and fish have made a very welcome return to the canals following a 15-year clean-up campaign. Dredgers keep the canal bottoms clear of debris – everything from abandoned bicycles to the cars of careless drivers who ended up in the water.

Until the IJsselmeer was dammed, the canals were flushed twice daily by natural tidal flow. Now a complex system of sluices and mechanical pumps does the job instead. Every night a third of the water in the canals is replaced by fresh water from the IJsselmeer. Excess water can also be pumped out if flood waters threaten the city after a period of heavy rain.

There are 160 separate canals in the city totalling 75km in length – spanned by 1,281 bridges, many of which are illuminated at night. Most of the bridges are fixed but several old wooden drawbridges remain, like the Magere Brug across the Amstel, topped by huge wooden balance beams that enable the central portion to be raised to admit tall-masted boats.

Nearly 5,000 people in Amsterdam live in 2,400 boats. These range from lovingly restored barges, gaily painted and bright with rooftop gardens, to utilitarian floating sheds. Living on a canal boat is not a cheap option; the cost of a boat and mooring is about the same as the rent for an equivalent sized flat, but for boat dwellers it is a deliberately chosen way of life. Some Amsterdammers consider the canals a wasted asset since little use is made of their transport potential. Perhaps this situation will change if the city ever gets round to banning the automobile.

Amsterdam's great phase of canal-building ended in the 17th century. Today the canals are quiet backwaters where people can relax on their houseboats, take strolls and simply stare into the water

Walk: The Old Side

This walk covers the oldest part of the city, the Oude Zijde (Old Side) district, often simply abbreviated to OZ. The area is also known to locals as Wallen (Walls), because the two main canals – OZ Voorburgwal and OZ Achterburgwal – once lay on either side of the medieval ramparts.

Allow 2 hours.

Start on Dam Square and walk across to the Grand Hotel Krasnapolsky, turning left down Warmoesstraat.

1 Warmoesstraat

Number 141 is the Condomerie Het Gulden Vlies (Golden Fleece) selling nothing but gift-wrapped condoms. Next door is an art gallery selling work by the squatters who live above – legally now, renting from the city council. Opposite is the **Effectenbeurs**, the modern Stock Exchange, housed in a building of 1913 decorated with tiles and patterned brickwork. Further down is the elegant Thee en Koffiehandel, an old-fashioned tea and coffee merchant. *Opposite this shop, turn right down Wijde Kerksteeg heading for the soaring tower of Oude Kerk.*

2 Oude Kerk

This lovely church (*see pp46–7*) is encrusted with chapels and little houses tucked up against the walls. Ironically, too, it is hemmed in by sex cinemas and the windows of prostitutes who operate within feet of this ancient place of worship, the city's oldest surviving monument. Oude Kerk (Old Church) was founded in the 13th century; it contains 16th-century vault paintings and fine stained glass as well as the grave of Rembrandt's wife, Saskia.

Return to Warmoesstraat, turn right and take the next street left.

3 Oudebrugsteeg

It is worth walking a short way down this alley to see the front of the Beurs van Berlage, and the Grasshopper Coffee Shop opposite. The latter bears an appropriate inscription, given its proximity to the former Amsterdam Exchange; the legend round the roof means 'nothing ventured, nothing gained'.

Return to Warmoesstraat, turning left, and continue until the street ends. Look left for a good view of the station, then turn right in Zeedijk.

4 Zeedijk

The first house on the left, No. 1, dates from 1550 and is one of only two medieval timber-framed houses left in Amsterdam (the other is in the Begijnhof). Opposite, the frieze above the doorway of St Olofskapel is carved with skeletons. At the first bridge, Oudezijds Kolk, the ancient lock still has its original gates and machinery.

Backtrack a short way from the bridge and turn left down Sint Olofssteeg, bearing left on to OZ Voorburgwal.

5 OZ Voorburgwal

Looking immediately to the left you will notice several 17th-century plaques, showing Noah's Ark and shipwrights' tools, that have been reset in the wall. Coming to the first bridge look right to No. 14, De Leeuwenburgh, a fine example of a step-gabled house dating from 1605. A short way further down on the right is No. 40, the Museum

Amstelkring. The attics of this and the two adjoining houses contain a *schuilkerkh*, a clandestine Catholic church, dating from the 17th century. At the next bridge look back for a good view of St Nicolaaskerk with its Neo-Baroque central dome. This harbourside church was built in 1885, shortly after the ban on Catholic worship in the city was lifted.

If you do not want to enter the red-light district, carry on up OZ Voorburgwal, past the Oude Kerk, to Damstraat, where you can turn right to return to Dam Square. Otherwise, continue over the bridge and on through Korte Niezel, then turn right on OZ Achterburgwal.

6 OZ Achterburgwal

This street is lined with sex shops and red-light windows, but looking upwards you will also see some of the city's most varied canalside architecture. Many would like to see the area cleaned up – these charming buildings would make highly desirable apartments. As it is, property owners can make so much money by renting ground floor rooms to prostitutes that they can afford to leave the rooms above unoccupied. For visitors with exotic tastes who want to sample the area after dark, Nos 106–8, the Theatre Casa Rosso, is one of the more 'respectable' nightclubs in the area.

Turn right into Oude Doelenstraat and you will see the Koninklijk Paleis in Dam Square straight ahead. Alternatively, you can continue exploring the area by going on to the next walk.

Will I be safe? Will I be shocked? These two questions worry anyone entering Amsterdam's infamous red-light district. The answer to both is a qualified yes. Take precautions against

theft and do not take photographs – there are plenty of gangland types about who want to remain anonymous, and your camera represents a threat. The shocks come more from the explicit contents of sex-shop windows than from the prostitutes themselves.

Despite the risks, the red-light district remains an essential part of the Amsterdam experience, as the large number of tour groups walking the area testify. As in every port city, commercialised sex has been available for centuries. Prostitutes operated here in the 17th century and paid rent to the city bailiff. He, therefore, had a vested interest in ensuring that they did not stray from the designated brothel area; if they did, he sent his drum and flute-playing guard to play outside the house in which they were ensconced until the combination of noise and exposure drove them back.

Today's red-light district is a pragmatic solution to a problem that will never go away. Under Dutch law, soliciting is illegal but what prostitutes and clients do in the privacy of their 'home' is regarded as their business – hence the

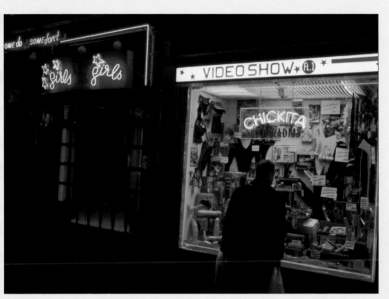

kamer te huur signs (rooms to rent); officially the money that changes hands is room rent, not payment for services rendered.

The prostitutes have, in most cases, chosen this way of life for its easy money. If they change their minds, there are numerous church and government agencies willing to provide support. Drug dealing and the worst excesses of pornography are more recent phenomena which the police and city authorities are trying to stamp out.

On the whole, the red-light district is colourful, it attracts tourists and contributes to the local economy, to the extent that brothel owners now sit on the Chamber of Commerce. There is a lighter side as well – the Condomerie

Het Gulden Vlies (Golden Fleece) has benefited from the post-AIDS boom in condom demand; it sells every kind imaginable – edible, luminescent or explosive.

Not perhaps for every visitor, but Amsterdam's red-light district is undeniably a tourist attraction. Amsterdam prides itself on a tolerant attitude to sexual tastes

Churches

While fringe religions flourish in Amsterdam, from Hare Krishna to New Age anthroposophy, conventional church-going has declined, leaving many of the city's churches forlorn, locked and redundant. The three main churches can be visited, however, and all of them are monuments of significant historical and architectural importance worthy of the city's reverence.

Westerkerk with its gold-topped tower

Nieuwe Kerk (New Church)

Nieuwe Kerk, on Dam Square, is run by a foundation which has decided to utilise the church for art exhibitions, concerts, lectures and even antiques fairs. Even so, it remains the national church of The Netherlands, used for the investiture of monarchs.

The church was first built in 1408: it is 'new' only in the sense that it is 200 years younger than the Oude Kerk (Old Church). It was gutted by fire in 1645, hence its furnishings date from the Golden Age, including a fine Baroque

The imposing Nieuwe Kerk on Dam Square

pulpit of 1649 carved by Aelbert Vinckenbrink; a magnificent organ case designed by architect Jacob van Campen, an ornate bronze choir screen and elegant wooden pews. National heroes commemorated include Admiral Michiel de Ruyter (d. 1676) whose magnificent monument dominates the choir.
Dam Square. Tel: (020) 638 6909; www.nieuwekerk.nl Open: during exhibitions only (phone to check, or consult website). Trams: 1, 2, 4, 5, 9, 13, 14, 16, 17 & 24. Nearby: Koninklijk Paleis (see pp54–5).

Oude Kerk (Old Church)

The city's oldest church was founded in the early 13th century. Pictures of ships feature everywhere, reminding us that the church is dedicated to St Nicolaas, the patron saint of sailors. The nave is ringed by numerous chapels sponsored by the city's powerful trade guilds. Richly coloured stained glass in the north choir, dating from 1555, depicts the Life of the Virgin. The door into the sacristy, where marriages were once certified, carries the motto: 'Wed in haste; repent at leisure'.

The tower has an especially tuneful carillon of bells, made in the 17th century, which is played every Saturday between 4pm and 5pm. You can climb the spire for views of the port and city. *Oudekerksplein 23. Tel: (020) 625 8284; www.oudekerk.nl Open: Mon–Sat 11am–5pm, Sun 1–5pm. Admission charge. Trams: 4, 9, 16, 24 & 25. Nearby: Amstelkring Museum (see pp26–7).*

Westerkerk (West Church)

Westerkerk, built by Hendrik de Keyser in the early 17th century, is renowned for two things: Rembrandt's grave and the tower. Rembrandt was buried in an unmarked pauper's grave, rediscovered by archaeologists during recent restoration work.

The tower is the tallest in Amsterdam at 83m. It is topped by the gold, red and blue crown of the Habsburg Holy Roman Emperor, Maximilian I.

The city gained the right to display the imperial crown in its coat of arms in 1489. According to one story, the privilege was granted after Maximilian I was cured of an illness after visiting Amsterdam's shrine of the Sacred Host. Others, more cynically, say he gave away his crown as a measure of his indebtedness to Amsterdam's bankers. *Prinsengracht 281, corner of Westermarkt. Tel: (020) 624 7766; www.westerkerk.nl Church open: Easter–Sept, Mon–Fri 11am–3pm; Jun–Jul also on Sat. Tower open: Apr–Sept, Mon–Sat 10am–5pm; Oct–Mar, arrange entry by calling (020) 689 2565. Admission charge for tower. Trams: 13, 14 & 17. Bus: 21. Nearby: Anne Frank Huis (see pp34–5).*

Concertgebouw

Johannes Brahms, who conducted his Third Symphony in Amsterdam in 1879, is reputed to have told his hosts: 'You are good people but bad musicians'. The remark spurred the city to set about creating a permanent orchestra and concert hall, both of which have since achieved worldwide acclaim. The Concertgebouw building ranks as one of the top three concert halls in the world, alongside Vienna and Boston. The building was designed by AL van Gendt and opened in 1888, an elegant Neo-Classical structure with reliefs of the Muses and celestial musicians. After subsidence, the building was restored for its centenary in 1988, and given a new glass foyer.

The resident orchestra, the Koninklijk Concertgebouworkest, achieved international renown under Willem Mengelberg and Bernard Haitink; now it is conducted by Riccardo Chailly. Other top orchestras perform here and the busy concert programme sometimes includes jazz as well as classics. *Concertgebouwplein 2–6. Tel: (020) 573 0511 (general enquiries); (020) 671 8345 (box office); www.concertgebouw.nl The best way to see the interior is to attend a concert; free lunchtime recitals are given on Wed. Box office open: daily 10am–7pm. Trams: 3, 5, 12 & 16. Nearby: Rijksmuseum, Stedelijk Museum, Van Gogh Museum.*

Electrische Museumtramlijn (Electric Tramline Museum)

The trams in the centre of Amsterdam seem to belong to another age, with their old-fashioned streetcar design and

jangling bells. They are, however, youngsters compared to the 60 or so historic trams that have been gathered together from all over Europe to create this transport museum, which is understandably popular with children. Most of the trams are static but some are used (see times below) to provide a service from Haarlemmermeer station to Amsterdamse Bos (Amsterdam Wood, *see p130*). Here you can alight for a picnic, a walk or a visit to the playground, farm reserve or Bosmuseum (Woodland Museum, *see p130*). Alternatively you can continue on through the 800-hectare park to the tram terminus at Amstelveen, a total journey time of 30 minutes.
Haarlemmermeer station, Amstelveenseweg 264. Tel: (info) 0900 423 1100; www.museumtram.nl

Outside the Concertgebouw

Open: Easter–Oct, daily 11am–5pm. Trams: 5, 6 & 16 (depart every 20–30 minutes from Haarlemmermeer station). Nearby: Amsterdamse Bos.

Heineken Browerij (Heineken Brewery)

A trip to the Heineken Brewery Museum (or Heineken Experience, as it is called nowadays) is more than just an indulgence for beer lovers; the former brewery has been turned into an excellent museum. The museum charts the invention of beer by the Sumerians, the origins of the first taverns and beer halls in Germany, the role of beer in festivities as depicted in the paintings of Brueghel and the vital importance of beer taxes to Amsterdam's medieval economy; vast quantities were consumed at the time simply because beer was a safer drink than water. Various parts of the brewing process are explained by audio-visual displays and the traditional white-tiled brewhouse is kept as spotless as it was when the brewery was operating.

Heineken finally closed the brewery in 1988 and relocated. It was a sad day for Amsterdam as beer had been brewed on the premises since 1592. Closure was inevitable as the Amsterdam plant could produce only 80,000 bottles an hour – less than Amsterdam alone consumes. The new plants have a staggering combined capacity of more than one million bottles an hour.
Stadhouderskade 78. Tel: (020) 523 9666; www.heinekenexperience.com Open: Tue–Sun 10am–5pm. Admission charge. Trams: 6, 7, 10, 16, 24 & 25. Nearby: Albert Cuypstraat (see p138).

Heavy horses at the Heineken Museum

ING Bank Building

The head office of the former NMB-PostBank (now the ING Bank) is an intriguing and imaginative building, worth seeking out in its suburban location by those interested in new architectural trends. The building, the most expensive ever built in The Netherlands, was completed in 1987. It was designed by Ton Alberts and Max van Huut in accordance with anthroposophical principles, a New Age philosophy in vogue with Amsterdam intellectuals that has been described as combining western humanist values with elements from eastern religions.

The building is designed to be 'organic'; none of the walls meet at right angles, a rejection of the alienating box-like form of most office blocks. Critics describe the result as a giant sandcastle – admirers compare it to ancient Inca architecture. Running water is a feature – the sound intended to have a calming effect – and there are numerous courtyard gardens.

The ING Bank building stands in ironic counterpoint to the nearby tower blocks of Bijlmermeer *(see p11)*. *Bijlmer 888. Tel: (020) 563 9111; www.ing.com Open: sometimes possible to take a guided tour (for details, contact Archivisie). Buses: 29, 59, 61, 137, 158, 174, 175 & 177. Metro: Bijlmer.*

Joods Historisch Museum (Jewish Historical Museum)

This museum is devoted to the history of the Jews in Amsterdam, a tragic story curtailed by the Nazi persecution of World War II. However, the museum is at pains to stress the continuity of Jewish life in The Netherlands.

The museum is housed in the former Ashkenazic synagogue complex, a series of 17th- and 18th-century buildings, and the displays cover three main themes. The first is concerned with the terror and persecution of the war, brought vividly to life by photographs and personal accounts. The second explains the Jewish religion, the major events in the calendar, its rituals and laws on diet and hygiene. Finally there is an account of the Jewish contribution to public life, politics and industry in Amsterdam, especially in developing the diamond industry.

The collection takes time to absorb, leaving visitors sober and reflective, but there is a lighter note – the excellent kosher café serves specialities such as almond *bolus* and *boterkoek* (buttercake). *Jonas Daniël Meijerplein 2–4. Tel: (020) 626 9945; recorded information (020) 625 4229; www.jhm.nl Open: daily 11am–5pm. Closed: Yom Kippur. Admission charge. Trams: 9 & 14.*

When Amsterdam was liberated from Nazi occupation on 5 May 1945, the city's Jewish population had fallen from 140,000 to fewer than 45,000. The survivors had lost everything – family, friends and homes. These stark facts are brought home by a visit to Jodenbuurt, the former Jewish Quarter, where only a handful of pre-war buildings still remain standing.

Among the first refugees to arrive in Amsterdam at the beginning of the 17th century were Sephardic Jews, who had been expelled from Spain and Portugal for refusing to accept Christianity. They built the huge Portuguese Synagogue (*see p53*) that dominates Mr Visserplein, between 1671 and 1675. Ashkenazic Jews from Germany and Poland soon followed; their synagogue complex on Jonas Daniël Meijerplein now houses the Jewish Historical Museum.

The statue of a burly dockworker stands between these two buildings. It was sculpted in 1952 by Marie Andriessen to commemorate a brave and singular act of defiance: in February 1941 the city's dockers and transport workers led a general strike in protest against Nazi treatment of the Jews. The strike, brutally suppressed, has gone down in Dutch history as the city's 'day beyond praise'.

Place names in the area perpetuate the memory of prominent Jews. Mr Visser was President of the Supreme Court of The Netherlands until he was dismissed by the Nazis; he played a prominent role in the Resistance until he died of natural causes. Jonas Daniël Meijer was a prominent 19th-century lawyer and a lifelong campaigner for Jewish civil rights.

MR. VISSERPLEIN
CENTRUM

Mr. Dr. L.E. VISSER (1871-1942)
RAADSHEER EN PRESIDENT HOGE RAAD DER NEDERLANDEN;
VERDEDIGDE DE BELANGEN VAN DE JOODSE BEVOLKING
TIJDENS DE DUITSE BEZETTING.

Despite everything, Jews still play an important role in the city's life. The van Moppes family sought refuge in Brazil during the war. They later returned to found one of the city's best-known diamond companies, the firm of A van Moppes & Zoon (*see p145*).

Facing page: Visitors to the Jewish Quarter study their whereabouts and are guided by clear street signs
This page: Inside and outside the Jewish Historical Museum – a living exhibition of Jewish faith and history

W a l k :   J o d e n b u u r t

Amsterdam's Jewish Quarter has been redeveloped since World War II but it contains several notable monuments, including Rembrandt's house.

Allow 1 hour.

Take the Metro from Amsterdam Centraal Station and alight at the first stop, Nieuwmarkt.

1 Nieuwmarkt Metro

Protestors battled with police on 'Blue Monday', 24 March 1975, to prevent the demolition of Nieuwmarkt houses to make way for the Metro. Murals and a giant demolition ball in the station recall that event.

Take the exit marked Nieuwmarkt/Sint Antoniesbreestraat and turn left down the latter street.

2 De Pinto Huis

Number 69 Sint Antoniesbreestraat is an Italianate house dating from 1605; now

a public library. Go in and look at the painted panels and ornate ceiling (*open: Mon & Wed 2–8pm, Fri 2–5pm, Sat 11am–2pm*). The house was built for Isaac de Pinto, a Jewish refugee from Portugal who became a wealthy banker. Popular protest prevented this building from being demolished in the 1970s when the rest of the street was redeveloped. Through the gate opposite there is a good view of the Zuiderkerk.

Just beyond this house, on the left, is a lock called Sint Antoniessluis. Look left for a good view of the Montelbaanstoren, built in 1512 as part of the city's defences, and of the warehouses lining Oude Schans. Turn round and you will see Rembrandt's house.

3 Museum het Rembrandthuis

This lovely house was built in 1606 (year of Rembrandt's birth) and cost the artist a huge 13,000 guilders when he bought it in 1639. Rembrandt was once hauled into court for cheating: he ordered wood to repair his house, and charged the cost to his neighbour, banker Isaac de Pinto. The banker sued, but the judge ruled that since de Pinto's name was on the bill, he must pay!

Turn right beside the Rembrandthuis, then left onto Waterlooplein where every day except Sunday you will find a flea market in full swing, a remnant of the old market of Jewish traders. Walk through the market to the huge church on the left.

4 Mozes en Aäronkerk

This vast Neo-Classical church dates from 1841 and many houses were demolished to make way for its construction, including the birthplace of Baruch Spinoza (1632–77), the Jewish philosopher.

Cross busy Mr Visserplein (named after LE Visser, the Jewish former head of the Dutch Supreme Court) to the massive brick synagogue on the left.

5 Portuguese Synagogue

When completed in 1675, this Sephardic synagogue was the biggest in the world. The interior is untouched. In the square outside, Marie Andriessen's Dokwerker statue commemorates the 1941 general strike led by dockers and transport workers to protest at Jewish persecution.

Cross Jonas Daniël Meijerplein (named after a remarkable lawyer who, at the age of 16 in 1796, became the first Jew to be admitted to the Dutch bar). Go to the synagogue complex opposite.

6 Joods Historisch Museum

The four buildings of the former Ashkenazic synagogue complex, now the Jewish Historical Museum, date from the mid-17th century. Walk through the connecting glass corridor for a glimpse of the museum. Sample kosher cakes in the museum café (*see p49*).

Leave by the main entrance, walk down Turfsteeg and cross Waterlooplein to the Stadhuis, aiming for the glass-covered arcade straight ahead.

7 Normaal Amsterdams Peil

The Normaal Amsterdams Peil arcade contains exhibits illustrating the standard ordnance datum adopted by Dutch surveyors in 1648.

Continue through the arcade. Turn left past the Muziektheater box office and Café Vienna. Leave the building by the doors straight ahead; look left at Blauwbrug, and right, down the Amstel, to Munttoren. Turn right for the black marble memorial slab for Jews who died in World War II. Follow Zwanenburgwal, alongside the Stadhuis, back to the Museum Het Rembrandthuis. The Metro entrance just ahead takes you back to Amsterdam Centraal Station.

Nearby

Only a stone's throw from the Portuguese Synagogue, on Plantage Middenlaan, is the entrance to Hortus Botanicus Plantage, the Botanical Garden. Beyond, in the leafy suburb of Plantage, visitors will find Amsterdam's zoo, Natura Artis Magistra.

Koninklijk Paleis

Royal Palace

The Royal Palace on Dam Square is Amsterdam's most prestigious architectural monument. It was built as an expression of civic pride between 1648 and 1655, when Amsterdam was at the peak of its power as a maritime trading city, capital of an empire stretching from the Americas to Australia.

Originally built as the Stadhuis or Town Hall, it was the one flamboyant structure in a city characterised by architectural restraint. There were practical reasons why Amsterdam had so few grandiose public buildings of any size: the soggy subsoil of mud and silt simply could not support any great weight of masonry.

The architect, Jacob van Campen, had to overcome this technical difficulty before he could fulfil his commission, to design the biggest town hall in all of Europe. He did so by creating a solid raft of timber piles, each 18m deep. The precise number of the piles – 13,659 – is known to every Amsterdam schoolchild because of a simple formula: to the number of days in the year (365) add 1 in front, and 9 behind.

Atlas shoulders the globe above the Royal Palace

On top of this raft, van Campen built the huge Neo-Classical edifice whose main façades are 80m long – just 2.13m more than the town hall of Antwerp, up to then the biggest in Europe. Amsterdam further signalled its supremacy over Antwerp, the city that had once been its major rival in the competition for maritime trade, by placing the figure of Atlas holding up the globe on the west front pediment; below, all the nations of the world are depicted offering up their goods to an allegorical female figure representing the city of Amsterdam. By contrast, the weathervane on top of the central cupola depicts the humble Dutch Koggeschip – the Dutch Cog – one of thousands of sturdy merchant ships that roamed the world bringing back the spices and tropical produce that made the city so immensely rich.

A notable feature of the Stadhuis is the lack of a formal entrance; puzzled visitors often wander round the block several times before discovering the small concealed doorway (on the right-hand side of the portico facing on to Dam square). There were good reasons for this: since the old city hall was stormed in 1535 by rioting Anabaptists declaring the imminent end of the world, and strikes and demonstrations were a regular feature of city life, such concealment helped seal the building from rioters. Besides, the basement of the town hall contained the city's prison, arsenal and bank vaults – according to historian Mark Girouard, up to 16 million Dutch florins could be stored in the vault at any one time, 'a foundation every bit as impressive as the famous 13,659 timber piles'.

Thus, the town hall had to be impregnable and the entrance was deliberately built small.

On the other hand, the Stadhuis was a public building, open to anyone who cared to enter. The ground floor housed the courts and council chamber as well as the offices of various city charities responsible for managing orphanages and hospitals. The upstairs was largely empty. In their desire for the biggest and best, Amsterdammers got more space than they could actually use.

In 1808 Napoleon invaded The Netherlands and put his brother on the throne. The Stadhuis was turned into the royal palace of today. As a result, the rooms contain an extensive collection of Empire furniture, but the most striking feature is the wealth of 17th-century marble sculpture, the work of Artus Quellin.

The sculpture is allegorical, indicating the use of each hall: Justice, Wisdom and Mercy decorate the tribunal or main courtroom; Venus is placed in the room where marriages were registered; and Icarus, falling from the sky, is in the office where merchants filed for bankruptcy. These playful and imaginative figures contrast with the

Amsterdam's most prestigious architectural monument

more ponderous paintings that decorate the walls and ceilings, but even these provide an insight into key moments in the city's history and the moral values of the Golden Age.

Today the palace serves as an occasional residence for Queen Beatrix, whose main home is in The Hague. *Dam 1. Tel: (020) 620 4060; (020) 624 8698 for guided tours; www.koninklijkhuis.nl Opening times vary. Telephone to check, or consult the website. Trams: 1, 2, 4, 5, 9, 13, 14, 16, 17, 24 & 25. Nearby: Nieuwe Kerk (see p46).*

Walk: The Golden Bend

The canal circle's Golden Bend was so named because of the size and splendour of the houses and the wealth of its former inhabitants.

Allow 1½ hours.

Begin on Dam Square. Walk to the left of the Koninklijk Paleis (Royal Palace) and cross the busy junction to walk down Raadhuisstraat.

1 Raadhuisstraat

This street was laid out in 1894, cutting a broad swath through the canal circle. The magnificent 19th-century building on the right, with its minaret-like

towers, was the main Post Office until 1991 when it was converted to form the Magna Plaza shopping galleria, worth a visit for a view of the galleried atrium. To the right, down Herengracht, is the ornate **Bartolotti House**, built in 1621 by Hendrik de Keyser for Guillielmo Bartolotti, a wealthy brewer and banker. Next door is the lovely Theatermuseum (partially lodged in the Bartolotti House) with its neck gables, dating from 1638. On the left-hand side of Raadhuisstraat is an attractive arcade designed by AL van Gendt, the same architect who built the Concertgebouw.

Turn left to walk down Keizersgracht.

2 Cross Streets

As you walk, it is worthwhile exploring the short cross streets to right and left, linking the three main canals. Their names indicate that this part of the city was once the haunt of furriers: Reestraat means Roe Street, *Harten* means deer, *Beren* bears. *Wolven* is clearly wolves, while Huidenstraat means Hide Street and Runstraat is named after the bark used in the leather tanning process.

Just after Berenstraat look for the huge building on the right inscribed 'Felix Meritis'.

3 Shaffy Theatre

This Neo-Classical building was founded in 1788 as a lecture theatre and concert hall by the Felix Meritis ('Happy through Achievement') Society, a patrician body whose aim was to promote knowledge of the arts and sciences. Haydn, Brahms and Grieg all conducted here. From 1946 it was the headquarters of the Communist Party, which was well supported just after World War II for its role in the Resistance. It was named after actor Ramses Shaffy. Now it is a part of the Felix Meritis complex, holding modern theatre performances.
At the next bridge turn left down Huidenstraat, and right down Herengracht.

4 Cromhouthuisen/Bijbels Museum

Numbers 364 to 370 on the right derive their name from Jacob Cromhout, a builder whose trademark (shown on a plaque near the door to No. 366) was a crooked stick, the literal meaning of his surname. Now the houses, dating from 1662, contains the Biblical Museum.
Continue down Herengracht. Stop to look at the succession of bridges marking the junction with Leidsegracht. Then take the first right, Leidsestraat.

5 Leidsestraat

A short way up on the right is Metz & Co, a department store founded in 1740. Despite its age, it sells ultra-chic modern furnishings. The rooftop café offers splendid views over central Amsterdam.
Carry on up Leidsestraat to Leidseplein.

6 Leidseplein

This is the centre of Amsterdam nightlife, with its mixture of up-market establishments and cheap fast-food outlets which have earned the square its nickname, 'La Place de la Mayonnaise'. On the right is the Stadsschouwburg (City Theatre), a venerable institution founded in 1894. Alongside is the eccentric Art Nouveau **American Hotel**, built in 1904 to the design of Willem Kromhout. Drop into the Café Americain to see its elegant stained glass, murals and Tiffany-style chandeliers. On the left-hand side of the square is 't Swarte Schaep (The Black Sheep), a restaurant dated 1627 and renowned for its Dutch-French cuisine. In the side streets to the right and left, respectively, are the city's two big rock music venues, Melkweg (in a converted dairy at Lijnbaansgracht 234A) and Paradiso (in a converted church at Weteringschans 6–8).
To return to Dam Square, backtrack down Leidsestraat, turn right down Herengracht which has the most splendid houses on the Golden Bend, now converted to consulates and bank premises. On the other side of the gracht is the Kattenkabinet (Cat Museum); worth visiting, not least for its interiors. Turn left in Vijzelstraat to reach Muntplein, then follow Kalverstraat all the way back to Dam Square.

Nearby
From Leidseplein it is a short walk to the renowned Rijksmuseum where you can also join The Museum Quarter walk (*see pp66–7*). Simply turn left in Leidseplein, alongside 't Swarte Schaep restaurant, down Korte Leidsedwarsstraat, a street lined with cafés and restaurants. At the end you will see Museumbrug (Museum Bridge) to your right, leading to the Rijksmuseum.

Kindermuseum (Children's Museum)

This museum is a separate branch of the Tropenmuseum (Tropical Museum, *see pp84–5*), which mounts special exhibitions for children and an imaginative range of hands-on workshop activities. The aim is to introduce young people to different cultures and ways of life. For example, they learn about life in the Asante Kingdom in Ghana by exploring clan staffs, stools, costumes, jewellery and drums from a reconstructed Asante palace. These events are meant for children from ages 6 to 12. Workshop numbers are limited, so book in advance – checking, too, to see whether the event is suitable for children who do not speak Dutch.

Of course, your children do not have to attend a workshop, the exhibitions are fun and educational in their own right. The programme takes 1½ hours, which parents (and children under six) can spend in the Tropenmuseum.
Linnaeusstraat 2. Tel: (020) 568 8215; www.kindermuseum.nl
Programmes: Wed afternoon, Sat–Sun, public & school holidays from the morning. Admission charge. Trams: 5, 7, 9 & 14 & bus 22. Nearby: Zoo (Artis).

Madame Tussaud Scenerama

If the Amsterdam Historical Museum is too dry for your tastes, try learning about the Golden Age of The Netherlands through the waxworks and tableaux of Madame Tussaud. In a romp through the 17th century, you will meet William of Orange and watch Rembrandt at work in his studio; enter a merchant's house, modelled on a painting by Vermeeer, and watch

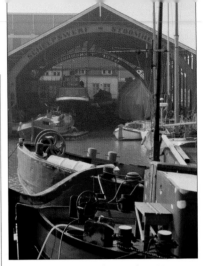

A sea-dog's paradise at the Kromhout Museum

children skating on the frozen canals of Amsterdam. Then the scene changes and you are back in the 20th century witnessing the first Moon walk and meeting famous politicians, pop stars and royalty. The wax figures move, you can watch yourself on TV shaking hands with world leaders and the special effects are laid on thick – all good fun if it is a cold, wet day, or your children are bored with art and architecture.
Dam 20. Tel: (020) 522 1010; www.madame-tussauds.nl Open: daily 10am–5.30pm (Jul–Aug 9.30am– 7.30pm). Closed: 30 Apr. Admission charge. Trams: 1, 2, 4, 9, 13, 14, 16, 17, 24 & 25. Nearby: Koninklijk Paleis, Nieuwe Kerk, Amsterdams Historich Museum (see pp32–3).

Museumwerf 't Kromhout (Kromhout Works Museum)

The Kromhout Works is the only remaining shipyard of the many that once filled Amsterdam's eastern harbour. Today it concentrates on restoring historic vessels.

The shipyard was founded in the 18th century by Diede Jansen Kromhout. It specialised in building iron vessels in the 19th century. The ornate glass and iron canopy that stands over the original slipway now shelters the working part of the museum where visitors can watch boats and engines being repaired.

The adjoining display area features models of steamers, shipwrights' tools and engravings of the docks in their heyday.

Hoogte Kadijk 147. Tel: (020) 627 6777; www.machinekamer.nl Open: Tue 10am–3pm. Admission charge. Buses: 22 & 32. Nearby: Nederlands Scheepvaartmuseum (Dutch Maritime Museum); Docklands (see pp76–7).

De Burcht (Vakbondsmuseum) (National Trade Union Museum)

A museum devoted to the history of the Dutch trade union movement does not sound especially appealing but, like several other museums in Amsterdam, it is the building that makes a visit worthwhile. In this case the building is the work of the Amsterdam School pioneer, HP Berlage. Known as the 'Berlage Castle', it was commissioned in 1900 as the headquarters of the General Dutch Diamond Workers' Union.

Its exhibits, mainly photographs, and documents relating to the rise of the Dutch labour movement, are outshone by the magnificent stairwell, with its Art Deco stained glass, tiling, bas-reliefs and murals by Dutch Impressionist RN Roland Holst.

Henri Polaklaan 9. Tel: (020) 624 1166; www.deburcht-vakbondsmuseum.nl Open: Tue–Fri 11am–5pm, Sun 1–5pm.

Closed: Mon, Sat & public holidays. Admission charge. Trams: 4 & 25. Nearby: Zoo (Artis), Hortus Botanicus Plantage (see pp130–31).

NEMO Science Centre

NEMO, the national science and technology centre, is located in a striking new building designed by Italian architect Renzo Piano. Interactive is the key word as the centre is full of push-button models that explain modern developments in science and technology – telephones, computers, holograms, cars, barcode readers and computer-aided design techniques.

Oosterdok 2, near the IJ Tunnel entrance. Tel: (020) 531 3233; www.e-nemo.nl (premium rate call). Open: Tue–Sun 10am–5pm (and Mon during school holidays). Admission charge. Bus: 22. Nearby: Nederlands Scheepvaart Museum.

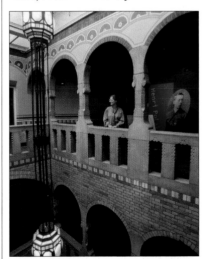

The Trade Union Museum is devoted to the working class

Museum Het Rembrandthuis

Rembrandt House Museum

The house in which Rembrandt spent the happiest and most successful years of his life is now a museum used to display an almost complete set of his etchings – 250 out of the 280 he is known to have made – along with drawings, personal memorabilia and period furniture. One room has an exhibition explaining the techniques of engraving, and the walls are hung with paintings by Rembrandt's pupils and by his teacher, Pieter Lastman.

The handsome Renaissance house was built in 1606. Rembrandt bought it in 1639, when he was 33 years of age. He had previously lodged in the same street, having moved to Amsterdam from his native Leiden in 1631. He soon became an acclaimed artist, able to count on an income from major commissions. Even so, he borrowed heavily to buy, furnish and maintain the house. This, and his lack of business acumen, contributed to his bankruptcy in 1656. In 1658, his creditors forced him to sell the house, though he was allowed to continue living in it until

Rembrandt at the Museum het Rembrandthuis

1660, when he moved to a cheaper home in the Jordaan district.

The house remains as it was in Rembrandt's day; the only subsequent change was the addition of a third storey with a classical pediment in place of the original step gable. Rembrandt and his household lived on the ground floor; the first floor served as his studio and the attic as the studio of his pupils. The house was then located on the edge of the city, in the fast-growing Jewish Quarter. Rembrandt chose the situation because the countryside was not far away.

The streets of the Jewish Quarter provided Rembrandt with a constant source of inspiration. His affection for low life characters can be seen in the famous series of engravings, hung in this museum, of beggars, vagabonds, organ-grinders and rat-catchers – he even portrayed himself in the guise of a beggar.

Among the other pictures displayed are views of Amsterdam and the surrounding countryside, several revealing self-portraits and etchings of the artist's parents, his wife and their son, Titus. A visit to the toilets is a must just for Rembrandt's drawings of a woman squatting in the bushes and a man standing in a pose of evident relief! *Jodenbreestraat 4–6. Tel: (020) 520 0400; www.rembrandthuis.nl Open: Mon–Sat 10am–5pm, Sun & public holidays 11am–5pm. Closed: 1 Jan. Admission charge. Trams: 9 & 14. Nearby: Joods Historich Museum (see p49).*

Rembrandt Harmenszoon van Rijn was born in Leiden in 1606, the eighth child of a prosperous corn miller who owned a mill close to the River Rhine, hence the family name. Rembrandt studied for a career in the law until he gave up university to concentrate on art.

He moved to Amsterdam in 1631 and the following year received his first major commission, *The Anatomy Lesson of Dr Nicolaes Tulp* (now in the Mauritshuis Museum, The Hague) portraying members of the city's guild of surgeons.

Fame and fortune followed, but so did personal tragedy. His wife, Saskia, died in 1642; three of their four children died in early childhood, leaving only Titus, whom Rembrandt adored. In that same year, despite Saskia's death, Rembrandt painted his best-known picture, *The Night Watch*.

This occupies the position of honour in the Rijksmuseum, but it was criticised in its time because some faces in the picture are partially hidden – the realism

we value was condemned at the time and his critics further accused Rembrandt of not following the 'rules of art', instead pursuing his own private insights.

He began to receive fewer commissions and, in 1656, was declared bankrupt. In 1660, he moved to a modest dwelling in Jordaan. Here he painted some of his greatest works, including the glowing and mysterious *The Jewish Bride* (Rijksmuseum). The sickly Titus died, aged 27, in 1668 and Rembrandt followed him less than a year later. In October 1669, he was buried in an unmarked pauper's grave (recently rediscovered) in Westerkerk, an ignominious end for a man now regarded as one of the greatest artists of all time.

One of the greatest artists of all time

Rijksmuseum I

The Rijksmuseum is one of Amsterdam's major highlights. The museum building is a vast Neo-Gothic palace with Burgundian towers and sculptural reliefs, designed by PJH Cuypers and completed in 1885. The national art collection of The Netherlands is in this museum, which contains a treasure-house of paintings, applied art, porcelain, silver and Asiatic sculpture. The museum is far too big to absorb in one visit: it pays to be selective.

Rijksmuseum is a treasure trove of national art

The Rijksmuseum is currently being renovated and much of it will be closed until 2008. However, about 400 of the highlights are still being shown in a special display in the Philips Wing, including many of the works covered in the following pages. The description here is based on the museum as it was when it was closed. When it re-opens in 2008, the layout will be different, but it is not yet possible to say what it will be like.

Rembrandt

For many visitors the Rijksmuseum means one painting, Rembrandt's celebrated *The Night Watch*. It can be seen by heading straight up to the first floor where the huge canvas is given pride of place at the end of the Gallery of Honour, in room 229. *The Night Watch* was named in the 19th century when experts believed the painting depicted a night scene. The layers of soot-blackened varnish have since been removed to reveal a quite different picture in which Rembrandt's dramatic use of sunlight and shade can be fully appreciated. Despite restoration, the old name has stuck, partly because the now-accepted title, *The Militia Company of Captain Frans Banning Cocq*, is such a mouthful.

The painting is an official portrait of one of the militia companies which acted as a combined police force-cum-army, ensuring law and order in the city and taking it in turns to mount a guard at the city gates. Each company had its own clubhouse and wealthier members paid for group portraits to adorn the walls. Hundreds of such portraits – the equivalent of today's group photographs – have survived, including those that hang in the Civic Guard Gallery of the Amsterdam Historical Museum.

Rembrandt's innovation was to break away from the static banquet scene or formal pose to show the militia company in action. Captain Cocq is giving his men the order to set off on a patrol of duty. He and his lieutenant are lit by a pool of sunlight while the militiamen behind are shown emerging from the shadowy gate of their clubhouse. The painting is full of movement as the men shoulder their weapons and form up into marching line, the dynamism enhanced by the play of light and the little girl caught up in the disorder. Her presence in the picture is a mystery; it is suggested that she may have been the daughter of the landlord of the militia clubhouse. The dead rooster hanging from her belt is an enigmatic pun (perhaps with bawdy connotations) on the name of Captain Cocq.

Rembrandt's contemporaries were not universally impressed by this work; some hailed it as a masterpiece of realism but far more censured him for failing in his fundamental duty as a portraitist to show the faces of each militiaman clearly. Instead, several faces are obscured by gesturing arms or shadow.

To the left of *The Night Watch*, rooms 212 to 217 contain further Rembrandt works, including two self-portraits – one painted at the age of 22 (in room 212), the other (*Self-Portrait as the Apostle*

Paul, in Room 217) in 1661 after bankruptcy had forced a major change in his lifestyle. In the same year, he painted the arresting *Bridal Pair*, also known as *The Jewish Bride* (in Room 217), a tender portrait of an unknown couple in glowing and heavily impasted reds and golds. Nearby (also in Room 217) is another masterpiece – *De Staalmeesters*. This depicts five inspectors of the Drapers' Guild and a hatless servant. From the way they look out of the picture it has been suggested that they are portrayed at a public meeting – someone in the invisible audience has addressed an unexpected question to them and their expressions, brilliantly highlighted by the muted black of their clothes, range from bemused tolerance to a rather lofty contempt.
Stadhouderskade 42. Tel: (020) 674 7047; www.rijksmuseum.nl Open: daily 10am–5pm. Closed: 1 Jan. Admission charge. Trams: 2, 5, 6, 7, 10, 16, 24 & 25. Nearby: Stedelijk Museum, Van Gogh Museum (see p67).

The Night Watch by Rembrandt at the Rijksmuseum

Rijksmuseum II

The Golden Age

Apart from the works of Rembrandt, the Rijksmuseum is noted for its collection of 17th-century works painted during the period of peace and prosperity known as the Golden Age of The Netherlands. They are displayed in rooms 211 to 219, beginning with the lively portrait of *Isaac Massa and his Wife* by Frans Hals. In this genial picture, the tubby and prosperous Isaac Massa leans back as if to show off his neat smiling wife, a paragon of fidelity as symbolised by the ivy clinging to the tree behind.

Hendrick Avercamp's *Winter Landscape* in room 211 and Jacob van Ruysdael's *Mill at Wijk by Duursteede* in room 218 are superb examples of the landscape painting for which Dutch artists are renowned.

Room 219 is devoted to the witty genre paintings of Jan Steen. Many of them depict the artist himself and his family in scenes of wild abandon, illustrating popular moralistic proverbs of the age – for example, *homo bulla*, or 'man is a bubble'. At first sight, *The Merry Family* looks like a happy domestic scene until you notice that the children are smoking, drinking, and being as licentious as their parents. The motto above the fireplace provides an ironic commentary; it says the young will sing the same old song, meaning that parents should beware of setting a bad example.

Quite different in tone altogether are the exquisite works of the Delft School hung in room 218, including four paintings by Vermeer and several by Pieter de Hooch. These simple paintings radiate peace and tranquillity, lending spiritual significance to the dutiful performance of the most ordinary domestic activities.

Dutch History and Asiatic Art

Rooms 102 to 112, on the ground floor, are used to display works that illustrate important aspects of Dutch history, even though they have no special artistic merit. They include portraits of key figures, such as William of Orange, historic battles at sea and on land, scenes of everyday life in the 17th century and, most fascinating of all, relics of colonial life in the East Indies, Ceylon, China and Japan.

From here it makes sense to continue the theme by visiting the Asiatic art collection in the basement of the Philips Wing, rooms 1 to 7. Here, among Indonesian sculptures and Hindu-Javanese architectural fragments, is the arresting figure of *Shiva, Lord of the Dance*, surrounded by a ring of fire. This 12th-century bronze from southern India is as stunning a work in its own way as the paintings upstairs, yet it receives far fewer visitors. The section ends with a comprehensive display of Chinese ceramics and some beautifully embroidered Japanese textiles.

Sculpture and Applied Art

This collection is organised chronologically, beginning with medieval and Renaissance art on the top floor, rooms 238 to 261. Some of the best exhibits consist of Romanesque and Gothic sculpture rescued from various abbeys and churches in The Netherlands. For fans of Delftware, rooms 255 to 257 contain a wealth of examples, including novelty items such as a birdcage, a violin and a pair of high-heeled shoes.

From room 260, a staircase leads to the ground floor where you may have to queue to get close to the popular doll's houses in room 164, made in the 18th century with exquisite attention to detail. The remaining rooms (162 to 181) illustrate Dutch interior design in the 18th and 19th centuries. This theme continues in the little-visited basement (rooms 24 to 34) which is worth seeking out for its outstanding collection of Empire and Art Nouveau furniture.

Later Dutch Art

Paintings of the 18th- to the early-20th century are displayed in Rooms 134 to 149, in the ground floor Drucker Extension. Most rewarding are the Impressionistic works of The Hague and Amsterdam Schools hung in the last three rooms – notably the atmospheric pictures of Amsterdam street life at the beginning of the 20th century painted by George Hendrick Breitner.

A close look at masterpieces in the Rijksmuseum

Walk: The Museum Quarter

This walk combines Amsterdam's three major museums with the best of the city's up-market shopping.
Allow 1½ hours.

Start at the Rijksmuseum. This is served by trams 2, 5, 6, 7 and 10 but a more enjoyable way to reach it is by Museumboat (departures every 30 or 45 minutes from 10am to 5pm daily from in front of Amsterdam Centraal Station; see also pp183–4).

1 Rijksmuseum

This palatial building was designed by PJH Cuypers in 1885 and bears a strong resemblance to his other great work, Amsterdam Centraal Station. Intended as a 'cathedral of the arts' it was built in Neo-Gothic style and embellished with sculptures, murals and tilework depicting various kinds of artistic endeavour.

The vast collection inside was begun in the 18th century by William V of Orange and later given impetus by Louis Napoleon who set up the Grand Musée Royal in the Koninklijk Paleis in a bid to make Amsterdam a major European centre for the arts.

Today the collection consists of 17 million works of art, including 5,000 paintings. Only 400 items are currently on display while the museum is renovated.

Walk under the echoing tunnel beneath the Rijksmuseum, the haunt of buskers, street traders and hot dog vendors, and turn right. Cross Jan Luijkenstraat and turn left on to Pieter Corneliszoon Hooftstraat.

2 PC Hooftstraat

At Amsterdam's most elegant shopping street, Dutch celebrities and the wealthy elite come to buy anything from Italian designer-label fashions, works of art or furnishings to just a box of handmade chocolates. Window shopping here is a pleasure, but should you get weary, you can rest your feet at one of the several elegant 'designer' cafés here.

After crossing Van Baerlestraat, continue up PC Hooftstraat to enter Vondelpark.

3 Vondelpark

This green oasis in the centre of the city was laid out in 1865 in the 'English' landscape style and named after the 17th-century Dutch poet, Joost van den Vondel, popularly known as the 'Shakespeare of The Netherlands'.

The days when the park was one vast hippy encampment are over but there are plenty of outdoor concerts – everything from classics to punk rock – and all other conceivable performances throughout the summer. The Nederlands Filmmuseum, to the right of the entrance, is a popular venue showing a wide selection of 'art' and historic films (*open: Tue–Thur 10am–5pm, Sat 11am–5pm, and in the evenings for shows*), and has a public film library (*open: Tue–Fri 1–5pm*). www.filmmuseum.nl

Retrace your steps down PC Hooftstraat and turn right in Van Baerlestraat. Take the second left, Paulus Potterstraat, for the other two big museums.

4 Stedelijk Museum and Van Gogh Musuem

The Stedelijk Museum houses the city's collection of modern art, though you would not guess so seeing the turreted red-brick building itself, built in Neo-Renaissance style in 1895. By contrast the Van Gogh Museum is stark and

ultra-modern. It was designed by Gerrit Rietveld and completed in 1973. Van Gogh's vibrant paintings inside are far more colourful than both buildings.

Continue down Paulus Potterstraat past Coster Diamonds (whose workshops can be visited daily 9am–5pm). Turn right, then left, passing through the Rijksmuseum tunnel. Cross the busy Stadhouderskade to reach Museumbrug (Museum Bridge) and head straight on for the Spiegelkwartier.

5 The Spiegelkwartier

This area can be considered an extension of the Museum Quarter but with a difference: the works of art on show here are all for sale. Many antique and fine art dealers set up shop here shortly after the Rijksmuseum opened in 1885 to capture the trade of visiting art lovers. Every shop along Spiegelgracht, Nieuwe Spiegelstraat and Kerkstraat is full of treasures and you can browse for hours.

Continue to the end of Nieuwe Spiegelstraat, past the Stichting de Appel, centre for modern art (temporary exhibitions open: Tue–Sun 11am–6pm; admission charge), then turn left on Herengracht, with its palatial bank and consulate premises. Take the first right, Koningsplein, which passes the floating flower market, the Bloemenmarkt, on the right. Bear left along Singel to see No. 425, the Militiegebouw (Militia Building), built in 1660 as the city arsenal and now the University Library. Take the next right, Spui, and the next left, Kalverstraat, to return to Dam Square.

John Evelyn, Samuel Pepys and other visitors to 17th-century Amsterdam were amazed by the quantity of fine art on sale. The first truly open market for art developed here, sold through dealers, bookshops and auctioneers. Instead of art being the preserve of rich patrons and institutions, ordinary citizens could commission portraits of their houses, possessions, friends or even of their prize animals (see Paulus Potter's *The Young Bull* in the Mauritshuis Museum, The Hague).

Amsterdammers were particularly fond of paintings with a coded message. Understanding the symbolism reveals that many of the Rijksmuseum's pictures are far more complex than they seem on the surface. Dogs, for example, represent gluttony and licentiousness, reflecting on the behaviour of the people in the picture. Golden vases, cut-glass decanters, musical instruments and peacock's feathers represent vanity. The frailty of human fortune is symbolised by eggshells or a fallen glass. Sometimes the paintings contain verbal puns: *vogelen*, the verb made of the noun *vogel'* (bird), is similar to the slang term for copulation, hence a man holding up a dead pheasant is saying more than you might at first suspect.

The paintings of the age therefore work in two ways; as representations of everyday life and as serious moral works. Jan Steen's bawdy tavern scenes in the Rijksmuseum are a warning against loose morals. Another of his works in the same museum has an innocuous title – *The Toilet* – yet it is full of erotic allusions: the candlestick, the sleeping dog, the red stockings (symbol of a prostitute) and the open jewellery box. Amsterdammers would know well how to read this as a warning against the prostitution of moral principles for mercenary ends.

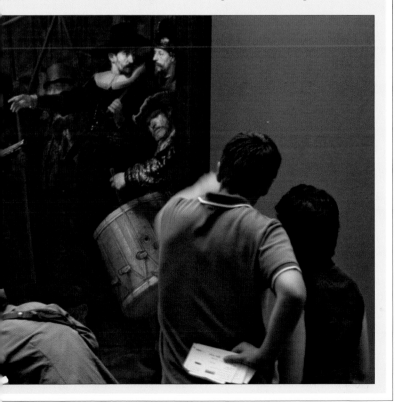

Viewing Rembrandt's *The Night Watch*

Van Gogh Museum

From the outside the Van Gogh Museum, designed by Gerrit Rietveld and completed in 1973, is a stark and unwelcoming building. Inside the huge whitewashed walls glow with the intense colours of Van Gogh's canvases. The collection, comprising some 200 paintings and over 500 drawings, was bequeathed to the city of Amsterdam by Van Gogh's nephew, also called Vincent. A selection of this work is displayed on the first floor – on the ground floor is the permanent collection of 19th-century art. The rest of the museum (including the spectacular new wing, designed by Kisho Kurokawa and opened in 2000) is used for temporary exhibitions that throw light on Van Gogh's achievement by comparing it with the work of his friends and contemporaries.

Van Gogh's work is presented in chronological order, beginning with his early studies of peasant life. These were painted in 1884–5 when Van Gogh was living at the family rectory in Nuenen, a village in Noord Brabant province surrounded by peat moorland. The colours of the soil are reflected in these sombre sketches of coarse faces and rough hands. *The Potato Eaters*, an early masterpiece, still has an arresting force, though Van Gogh explained, in a letter to his brother Theo, that he did not intend to

present rural life as brutalised and backward; 'I have tried to make it clear' he wrote, 'that those people, eating their potatoes in the lamplight, have dug the earth with those very hands they put in the dish, and so it speaks of manual labour, and how they have honestly earned their food.'

The next section covers Van Gogh's time in Paris (1886–8) and his various experiments with *pointillisme* and the light, airy style of the Impressionists. The next section, covering his period in Arles (1888–9) shows a

Van Gogh's artistic career lasted a mere 10 years, yet he painted over 2,000 works – 200 alone in the 15 months he spent in Arles. Painting was a passion ('one works without being aware', he wrote) and he would even work all night with candles stuck around the rim of his hat.

Van Gogh sold only one painting in his life; he was so poor that his diet consisted of meagre amounts of bread and more copious amounts of coffee and alcohol. Chronic undernourish-ment and lack of sleep may have contributed to his mental breakdown. In a famous quarrel he threatened his friend Gauguin with a knife and then, in a fit of remorse, cut off his own ear. He admitted himself to an asylum but not long afterwards, aged 37, he shot himself.

Only after his death were his talents appreciated and his works now command world-record auction prices.

sudden transformation in his work. The paintings of this period are extraordinarily vivid and intense, and the colours are stunning – the blazing yellows and oranges of *Sunflowers*, the brilliant white of peach blossom against a turquoise spring sky, the blues and yellows of harvest scenes and landscapes all speak of Van Gogh's enthusiasm for 'the full effect of colour'.

The two final sections of the museum show the pictures he produced while staying at the St Remy asylum (1889–90), after the famous ear-cutting incident, and in the last weeks of his life when he stayed at Auvers before committing suicide. These paintings fluctuate between tortured abstract depictions of twisted tree roots and flashes of Van Gogh at his most accomplished – *Irises*, for example, was dashed off in a moment of inspiration between the bouts of depression that finally brought the brief life of this visionary artist to an end.

Paulus Potterstraat 7. Tel: (020) 570 5200; www.vangoghmuseum.nl Open: daily 10am–6pm (10pm Fri). Closed: 1 Jan. Admission charge. Trams: 2, 3, 5 & 12. Nearby: Rijksmuseum, Stedelijk Museum.

Playground outside the starkly modern building of the Van Gogh Museum

Nederlands Scheepvaartmuseum

The Netherlands Maritime Museum is housed in a massive Classical building on the waterfront which was built in 1656 as the warehouse and arsenal of the Amsterdam Admiralty. Here the provisions of the Dutch navy were stored. The Admiralty employed a huge task force of cats whose job was to patrol the stores looking for rats and mice.

Graceful exhibits in the Maritime Museum

The sheer size and scale of the building can be judged by the fact that it now accommodates several very large historic vessels, as well as evocative paintings and maps and globes, all of which help tell the story of the Dutch maritime achievement; the story is covered exhaustively, from ancient Roman ships to luxurious modern passenger liners and leisure craft.

Perhaps the most interesting part of the museum covers the Golden Age. The first Dutch expeditions to the Spice Islands – modern Indonesia – set sail in the 1590s. Their aim was to chart navigable routes to the East Indies, via the Cape of Good Hope and the Indian Ocean. Reliable sea maps underpinned the rapid rise of The Netherlands as a trading nation. Among collectors of early maps, the names of Dutch cartographers such as Blau and Jansson are held in reverence for the accuracy and beauty of their work. The maps and globes displayed in the Maritime Museum are equally fascinating because they show, step by step, the charting of hitherto unexplored islands and

continents such as Australia (then called New Holland), Tasmania, China, Japan and the coast of South America.

Amsterdam's shipbuilders also led the world, which is why Sir Walter Raleigh, Samuel Pepys and Tsar Peter the Great all visited, looking for ideas that would benefit the English and Russian navies. The museum explains the development of the sturdy three-masted merchant vessels of the 16th century which sailed in search of spices and luxury goods and of the powerful warships of the Dutch fleet used to defend the nation's commercial interests.

The first merchant voyages were financed by private entrepreneurs who, in the main, reaped a rich reward. In 1602 it was decided that Far East trade should be co-ordinated, and numerous small companies joined forces to create the Dutch East India Company. This was funded by an innovative public share flotation and the company's charter gave it almost unlimited powers.

By 1669 it was synonymous with Dutch colonial power; it employed a private army and owned a huge fleet of warships and merchant vessels, having established trading outposts stretching from South Africa to the Japanese island of Deshima.

The Dutch West India Company was founded in 1621 with similar powers, to co-ordinate trade with West Africa and the Americas. It was less successful, suffering intense competition from the English, Spanish and Portuguese.

One of its colonies, established on the island of Manhattan, was captured by the English in 1664, and its name changed from New Amsterdam to New York.

The museum's account of the rise and fall of these two powerful trading companies is fascinating, but there are plenty of other diversions. Children especially will admire the gilded royal barge (made in 1818 for King William I), and the reconstructed East Indiaman (the *Amsterdam*), moored in the dock outside the museum, is alone worth the price of the entrance ticket. Climbing aboard this ship, whose crew consists of actors, you gain a very real sense of the bravery of sailors who plied the oceans in a such a vulnerable construction of wood and sailcloth.

Kattenburgerplein 1. Tel: (020) 523 2222; www.scheepvaartmuseum.nl
Open: Tue–Sun & public holidays 10am–5pm, mid-Jun–mid-Sept, daily 10am–5pm. Closed: 1 Jan, 30 Apr & 25 Dec. Admission charge. Buses: 22 & 32. Nearby: Docklands (see pp76–7), Museumwerf 't Kromhout.

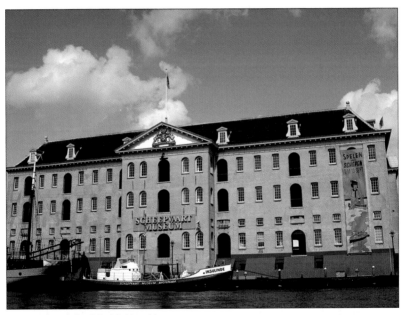

The waterfront bulk of the Maritime Museum

Dutch maritime expansion in the 17th century turned Amsterdam into the world's biggest market for tropical goods. Contemporary visitors wrote of the harbour bustling with hundreds of ships so that they first glimpsed the city through a forest of masts and rigging. Timber causeways and floating wooden cranes stretched far out into the harbour. Strangers arriving after dark, when they were not allowed into the city, were lodged in one of two purpose-built floating inns. Visitors were impressed by the sheer noise of the Beurs, the commodities exchange, where Muscovites, Persians, Turks, West Indians and traders from scores of other nations haggled over the price of sugar and spices, silks and Chinese porcelain. The city's own merchants were helped by the Bank of Amsterdam, founded in 1609, which offered loans at rates of only three or four per cent interest. With this ready source of cheap money, merchants could speculate, buying goods cheap and warehousing them until prices rose.

Warehouses remain the most visible legacy of the era. Though since turned into apartments, many retain their huge shuttered doors and pulley wheel in the gable. A maze of pipes inside carried water from rooftop cisterns for use in the event of fire – the origin of modern sprinkler systems. There are other reminders of the era in the palatial headquarters of the Dutch East India Company and the Schreierstoren (Tower of Tears), where sailors took leave of their wives and girlfriends before departing overseas. Sadly, though, Amsterdam lost its maritime atmosphere in the 1880s when the old harbour was filled in to build Centraal Station, thus signalling the end of the city's long and profitable relationship with the sea.

Facing page: The Maritime Museum tells the story of the first merchant voyages
Above: Most of the city's elegant canalside houses and warehouses were built in the 17th century; the hoists are still necessary for moving furniture since the narrow buildings only have narrow staircases; right: the Schreierstoren (Tower of Tears)

Walk: The Docklands

Discover the remains of maritime Amsterdam in an area of
the city which visitors rarely penetrate.
Allow 2 hours.

*Start from Amsterdam Centraal Station
and walk left, past the VVV Informatiekantoor (tourist information centre),
along Oosterdokskade. Use the pedestrian
crossing to reach the other side of Prins
Hendrikkade, and turn right.*

1 Schreierstoren

You will soon reach the 'Tower of Tears',
built between 1480 and 1488 as part of
the city wall (interior not open to the
public). By tradition sailors' wives
watched their husbands' ships depart

here. There are several plaques: one
reads 'Eerste Schipvaart Naar Ostindie
1595' (First Voyage to the East Indies,
1595), another records that Henry
Hudson's ship, the *Half Moon*, set out
from here in 1609 on a voyage which
discovered the Hudson River and
Manhattan Island.
*Look right for a good view of Zuiderkerk,
then continue round Prins Hendrikkade.*

2 Scheepvaarthuis

The next building on the right is

Maritime House, a richly decorated building and the best example of Amsterdam School architecture in the city. It was built by the Brothers Van Gendt between 1913 and 1916 and is covered with fanciful brick sculptures.
At the far end of the building turn right down Buiten Bantammerstraat and cross the bridge with its seahorse motifs. Turn left down Oude Waal and head for the tower at the end.

3 Montelbaanstoren

This tower was built in 1512 when the city's defences were extended to run up the side of the Oude Schans ('Old Bulwark') basin. The openwork spire was added in 1606 by Hendrik de Keyser.
Turn left up Kalkmarkt, noting No. 8 with its steamship plaque, right on Prins Hendrikkade and right down 's Gravenhekje, noting the West India Company warehouse to the left (1642). Turn left down Rapenburg. An ugly, but unavoidable, stretch lies ahead, caused by the entrance to the IJ tunnel (notice the magnificent ship-like curved building of the NEMO Science Centre), which links the city to its northern residential area. Turn right, cross the tunnel sliproad by the pedestrian lights, walk to the right of the fire station down Anne Frankstraat, then left down Nieuwe Herengracht. Walk past the lock on Rapenburgerplein, turn right across the next bridge and right through a monumental arch inscribed Entrepôtdok.

4 Entrepôtdok

This vast complex consists of 84 warehouses, dating from the 19th century, which have been converted to apartments, named in alphabetical order after Dutch cities.
At the end, turn left, climb the steps and cross the bridge to the right for a view of the Museum of Kromhout. Go back over the bridge, walking down Hoogte Kadijk, and take the first right, Overhaalsgang. Cross the footbridge, looking right for a view of the De Gooyer Funenmolen (windmill).

5 Oosterkerk

On the opposite side of the road from the footbridge is the Oosterkerk, built in 1670 to serve the local shipbuilding community. The church stands on a man-made island, Wittenburg. There is another island to the right (Oostenburg), and a third to the left (Kattenburg). All these man-made islands date from 1650 and were constructed to provide dockyards where the warships of the Dutch navy were built.
Turn left in front of the church and walk down to the former Zeemagazijn.

6 Nederlands Scheepvaartmuseum

The Zeemagazijn, or Admiralty arsenal, was built in 1656 and now houses the outstanding Netherlands Maritime Museum. This is well worth a visit, especially to explore the East Indiaman, the *Amsterdam,* moored in the dock alongside, to experience something of life aboard a typical 17th-century cargo ship (*see pp72–3*).
To return to Amsterdam Centraal Station, catch bus 22 or 32 from Kattenburgergracht. The alternative is a rather dreary walk along traffic-choked Prins Hendrikkade.

Walk: Jordaan

Jordaan is the sock-shaped district wrapped round the western half of the canal circle. Despite its name (*jordaan* means garden), this was the industrial quarter of 17th-century Amsterdam where noxious trades were carried on. Once a slum, it is now a friendly neighbourhood of inexpensive shops and cafés, and numerous hidden almshouses (*hofjes*).
Allow 1½ hours.

From Dam square walk down Raadhuisstraat past Westerkerk and over

the bridge to the left bank of Prinsengracht. Walk down this canal and take the second left, Bloemgracht.

1 Bloemgracht
The Flower Canal is also known as the Herengracht (Gentlemen's Canal) of the Jordaan because it has the most splendid houses. The step-gabled buildings, Nos 87–91, date from 1642, and belong to an organisation dedicated to preserving the many ornate buildings in this area designed by the Golden Age architect Hendrik de Keyser.
At the second bridge turn right into Tweede Leliedwarsstraat.

2 Tweede Leliedwarsstraat
Craft shops and art galleries line this short street with the formidable name which means 'Second Lily Cross Street'. All the short intersecting streets are numbered from east to west: Eerste (First), Tweede (Second) and so on, and all the main streets are named after flowers.
Cross Nieuwe Leliestraat and take the next left.

3 Egelantiersgracht

The beautifully named Eglantine (Honeysuckle) Street has a well-restored almshouse, Sint Andrieshofje, at Nos 107–114, dated 1617, one of the oldest in the city. Enter to see a remarkable Delft-tiled passageway with a hidden garden. From outside the building turn round and walk up the canal, noting the plaques of No. 89, two tailors at work, and Nos 61–3, a hooded hawk. Plaques like these, often relating to the householder's profession, were once used to identify houses.

At the next bridge look right for a good view of Westerkerk, then turn left down Tweede Egelantiersdwarsstraat. There are scores of excellent shops along this street. Turn right in Egelantiersstraat and look for the almshouse entrance at No. 52.

4 Claes Claeszoon Hofje

This almshouse consists of 23 smaller houses dating from 1620 which display a fine sequence of gable styles.

Turn left in Eerste Egelantiersdwarsstraat and left again in Tuinstraat. Halfway up on the left is Regensboog-Liefdehofje, with 17th-century step gables. Take the next right, Tweede Tuindwarsstraat, cross Anjelierstraat (Carnation Street) then continue down Ze Anjelierdwarstraat and Tichelstraat, and turn right in Karthuizerstraat.

5 Huys Zillen Weduwen Hofje

This street is dominated by the long façade of the 1650 almshouse – the 'House of the Elderly Widows' – the biggest and best of the Jordaan *hofjes*. *Return to Tichelstraat, looking left for a last view of Westerkerk. Turn right onto*

Lijnbaansgracht and walk down this canal, past the iron lifting bridge on Willemsstraat. Turn right in Palmgracht.

6 Palmgracht

Here are several more fine houses. Nos 73–79, on the right, date from 1673, and their plaque depicts a bunch of radishes. On the left, at Nos 28–38, is the Boffschehofje, founded in 1648 by Pieter Adriaenszoon Raep, whose surname means turnip, hence the vegetable depicted on the plaque.

At the end of Palmgracht turn right on to Brouwersgracht. Follow this canal, with its numerous bridges, boats and waterfowl, all the way back to the centre of Amsterdam, heading for the copper-green dome of the Lutheran Round Church (see p36) visible in the distance.

Hofjes

Many of the *hofjes* in the Jordaan district were built by wealthy merchants for housing sick or retired employees and their families. The pensioners were expected to work in return for this charity and the characteristic inner courtyard was originally used as a *bleekveld*, a bleaching field, for laying out cloth to bleach in the sun. Many are now beautifully planted communal gardens.

Old houses border the quiet Egelantiersgracht

Spaarndammerburt

The Spaarndammerburt housing estate is one of the most characteristic examples of the work of the famous Amsterdam School, a group of idealistic architects who worked in the city from 1911 to 1923. Their work was stimulated by the 1901 Housing Act under which the municipality was empowered to build subsidised 'council housing'.

This group of architects responded with distinctive and ornamental buildings, a far cry from the box-like housing units of a later age. One of their fundamental beliefs was that the souls of the working-class occupants should be stimulated by presenting them with architecture of great aesthetic beauty.

The buildings of Spaarndammerburt make great use of deep sweeping roofs of terracotta tile, of patterned brickwork, sculpture and whimsical detail. The needle-like spire rising from the buildings on Hembrugstraat serves no purpose other than to enliven the roofscape. Straight lines are avoided in favour of gracious curving façades and window frames, giving the buildings a ship-like appearance. The architects planned every detail, down to the letter boxes and the type-style used for house numbering. These photogenic buildings are a joy to visit – modern, yet reminiscent of the intimate *hofjes*, or enclosed courtyards, of medieval Amsterdam.

Spaarndammerburt lies to the northwest of the Jordaan district. The best buildings are bounded by Zaanstraat, Hembrugstraat and Oostzaanstraat. Bus: 22. Nearby: the Western Islands (see Unknown Amsterdam, *pp90–91).*

Stadhuis/Muziektheater Complex

These public buildings, on the edge of the redeveloped Jewish Quarter, are known to Amsterdammers as the Stopera complex – a contraction of Stadhuis (City Hall) and Opera, but also an ironic reference to the 'Stop the Opera' campaign of the 1970s and early 1980s. Controversy surrounded these buildings from the start because of the cost (300 million

AMSTERDAM'S NEW SOUTH

Many of the buildings in the Nieuw Zuid (New South) were designed in the distinctive Amsterdam School style by Michel de Klerk and Pieter Kramer. If you like this style of architecture, take tram 4 from Centraal Station, alight at Rooseveltlaan and explore the triangular area bounded by Churchillaan to the north (the rather ugly 12-storey block in the apex of the triangle has the dubious honour of being Amsterdam's first skyscraper, built in 1935).

Another oasis of playful Amsterdam School work is the estate called De Dageraad (The Dawn), completed in 1923. To find it, continue north from Churchillaan, up Waalstraat, to PL Taaksstraat.

guilders, which activists would have preferred to see spent on housing and other social needs), the inclusion of an opera, and ballet theatre (regarded as elitist) and the fact that numerous houses which had been taken over by squatters were demolished to clear the site.

Despite violent protests the buildings went ahead and were completed in 1988. The controversy lingers, but in more muted form; critics regard the complex as an ugly eyesore that is out of scale with the surrounding canalside houses. The **Muziektheater**, with its white marble cladding, is dismissively nicknamed 'the set of dentures'. It is home to The Netherlands Opera and National Ballet companies, but continues to be dogged by poor acoustics, despite expensive attempts to remedy the problem.

Aidan School in Spaarndammerburt

Sculpture at the Muziektheater

Visitors to Amsterdam should see the complex – indeed, it is hard to miss – and make up their own mind. You can take advantage of free lunchtime concerts given between September and June. From the inside the huge plate-glass windows frame superb views.

The arcade linking the two parts of the complex has a mural showing a cross-section through The Netherlands to illustrate Normaal Amsterdams Peil (Normal Amsterdam Level) the standard ordnance datum by which heights are measured in this country where half the land lies below sea level.

Muziektheater: Amstel 3. Tel: (020) 625 5455 (box office); www.muziektheater.nl Open: daily 10am till performance starts, Sun & public holidays from 11.30am. Guided tours: Sat 3pm. Free admission but there is a charge for guided tours (book in advance for English-language version). Stadhuis: Amstel 1. Tel: (020)

552 9111. Guided tours first Mon of the month at 11am. Admission charge. Trams: 9 & 14. Nearby: Waterlooplein Flea Market (see p138), Museum Het Rembrandthuis.

Stedelijk Museum

Amsterdam's modern art museum has always been a great complement to the other two main museums in the Museum Quarter, the Rijksmuseum and the Van Gogh Museum. However the building, which dates back to 1895, is at present being renovated, and with the Rijksmuseum partially closed, the Museum Quarter has been effectively halved.

Currently the best of the Stedelijk's collection is still on display, but you will need to go to its temporary home to see it. This is the old post office building near the Centraal station, the Post CS, which is itself in the process of being redeveloped.

As this happens, it is giving shelter for a while to the modern art collection on two floors, the cutting-edge W139 Gallery in the basement, and the chic club-restaurant Eleven, which offers fabulous city views from its eyrie at the top of the building.

The Stedelijk will probably only be here till some time in 2006, and as its own home won't be ready for occupation until 2008, at the current rate of progress, it may well have another home till then and visitors will need to ask around for the details.

One reason for the renovation is to make better use of the space, as there has never been room to show more than a part of the collection, which covers the period from 1850 to the present day. Many of the big names in modern art are represented, though not always with well-known works. These in themselves often shed new light on a particular artist to the average visitor not thoroughly familiar with their life's work.

Names such as Cézanne, Chagall, de Kooning, Lichtenstein, Matisse, Mondriaan, Picasso and Andy Warhol all draw the crowds, but often it is the more striking examples of contemporary works which catch the eye. One of the permanent exhibits has always been a room devoted to the work of the Russian artist, Kasimir Malevich. The works were chosen by the artist himself and the accompanying text explains his personal evolution from realism, through cubism to Suprematism, a form of art that is concerned with the essence of colour, form and technique rather than representation. It will be interesting to see how these, and the other great works from the collection, are displayed in the new building.

Temporary Home: Post CS, Oosterdokskade 5. Tel: (020) 573 2911 (general enquiries); (020) 573 2737 (recorded information).

Trams: 1, 2, 4, 5, 6, 9, 13, 16, 17, 24 & 25.

Permanent Home: Paulus Potterstraat 13. Tel: (020) 573 2911 (general enquiries); (020) 573 2737 (recorded information); www.stedelijk.nl Open: ring or check website for new opening hours. Trams: 2, 3, 5 & 12.

Displays at the Stedelijk Museum are currently on the move

Theatermuseum

The Theatre Museum is housed in a
splendid 17th-century building, which is
worth seeing in its own right. The house
was purchased in 1638 by Michael Pauw,
founder of the Dutch West India
Company, and transformed by the
leading Golden Age architect, Philip
Vingboons. For the façade of the
building, Vingboons designed the first
ever 'neck gable', so called because of its
resemblance to the neck and shoulders
of a wine bottle. The device was to prove
popular and was widely copied by other
Amsterdam architects.

The murals and ceiling paintings of
the interior, depicting landscapes
and biblical subjects, date from a
refurbishment in 1728, and are the work
of the leading artists of their day, Jacob
de Wit and Isaac de Moucheron. These
are complemented by lavish stucco work
and a magnificent spiral staircase.

The museum itself tells the history
of Dutch theatre from the 17th century
up to the modern age of TV, film and
video, through a range of fascinating
changing exhibits. These include a
miniature theatre dating from 1781, a
fine costume collection, props, books,
drawings, prints, models illustrating the
backstage work of scenery, lighting and
stage effects, including wind, rain and
thunder machines. There is also a
garden where tea is served, a popular
meeting place for actors, writers and
directors.
*Herengracht 168. Tel: (020) 551 3300;
www.tin.nl Open: Mon–Fri 11am–5pm,
Sat–Sun & public holidays 1–5pm. Closed:
1 Jan, 30 Apr & 25 Dec. Admission charge.
Trams: 13 & 17. Bus: 21.*

The Theatre Museum

Tropenmuseum (Tropical Museum)

The Tropical Museum is housed in one
of the city's most charming buildings,
the former Dutch Colonial Institute, a
whimsical structure of minaret-like
towers designed in the 'eclectic' style and
completed in 1923. The façades are
decorated with reliefs depicting the
peoples of the East, the cultivation of
the most important crops of the former
colonies – rubber, tobacco, sugar and
rice – and four of the major world
religions, Hinduism, Islam, Christianity
and animism, the belief that inanimate
and natural phenomena have souls.

The museum was transformed in the
1970s from a celebration of Dutch
imperialism to something altogether
more exciting. The museum now
illustrates life in the tropics and
subtropics: India, Southeast Asia and
South America are brought to life
through colourful and authentic
reconstructions of huts, houses, bazaars
and shops, complete with characteristic

smells; only the heat and flies are missing, and background tapes play continuously to evoke the noise and bustle of the streets.

Visitors wander in and out of the displays making their own discoveries. One minute you are wending your way through crowded Arab alleyways, the next you are out on the African savannah, caught in a thunderstorm. It is easy to lose yourself for hours, especially if you settle down to watch some of the documentary video tapes dealing with Third World problems, such as rainforest depletion and population growth.

The museum hosts numerous cultural events and also has a theatre, the Soeterijn, with an evening programme of non-Western music, theatre and dance from visiting performers. There is also a restaurant, the Ekeko, which serves up typically tropical snacks, lunches and evening meals. There is a separate museum for children (*see* Kindermuseum, *p58*) though there is much to interest especially the older child in the Tropenmuseum.

The museum shop stocks a range of exclusive handmade arts and crafts from the tropics and subtropics. The colourful Dappermarkt (market) is just a short walk away.

Linnaeusstraat 2. Tel: (020) 568 8215; www.tropenmuseum.nl
Soeterijn Theatre: (020) 568 8500.
Open: daily 10am–5pm. Closed: 1 Jan, 30 Apr, 5 May & 25 Dec. Admission charge. Trams: 9, 10 & 14. Bus: 22. Nearby: Zoo (Artis).

The world explored at the Tropical Museum

Walk: Around the Amstel

Amsterdam is named after the River Amstel which once flowed through the heart of the city. The original course has since been filled in but on this walk visitors will see the stretch that survives, a broad rolling watercourse that brings the canal circle to an abrupt end in the east of the city.

Allow 1 hour.

Start at Muntplein. Its landmark tower, the Munttoren, was given its elegant steeple by Hendrik de Keyser in the early 17th century. Cross the chaotic junction and walk down Reguliersbreestraat to the cinema halfway down on the right.

1 Pathé Tuschinski

This wonderful Art Deco cinema stands incongruously surrounded by fast-food outlets and tacky souvenir shops. Founded by Abram Tuschinski, a Polish Jew who died at Auschwitz, it opened in 1921 and retains all its original fittings – go inside to admire the lavish carpets, murals and lamps of the foyer, and to check what films are showing.

Turn right out of the cinema for Rembrandtplein.

2 Rembrandtplein

A statue of Rembrandt, on the right, looks down with a bemused expression on the square that bears his name. The square is completely surrounded by pavement cafés; though commercialised,

it is nevertheless a lively spot at night.
Walk down Amstelstraat, passing the
formal gardens of the Museum Willet-
Holthuysen on the right, to the Amstel.

3 Amstel

Straight ahead is the unmissable bulk of
the Stadhuis/Muziektheater complex,
considered by locals to be a blot on the
landscape (at least regarding the Town
Hall) and completed in 1986. Alongside
is the Blauwbrug of a century earlier,
modelled on the flamboyant Pont
Alexandre III in Paris. This is a more
restrained version with boat-shaped
piers and lampstands topped by the
imperial crown of Amsterdam's coat of
arms. On the opposite bank, to the
right, you will see the long façade of the
Amstelhof, built in 1683 as a home for
the elderly and still used as such.
Turn right and follow the Amstel
embankment to the first bridge.

4 Herengracht

Look right from the bridge down this
leafy canal with its patrician houses. If
you have the time walk down the right-
hand embankment to visit the Museum
Willet-Holthuysen, No. 605, and see its
authentic and stately 18th-century
interiors.
Continue along the Amstel, past No. 218
which houses the Six Collectie, heading for
the white lifting bridge spanning the river.

5 Magere Brug

The 'Skinny Bridge' is over 300 years old
and derives its name from an earlier,
even narrower, bridge across the Amstel.
This has become one of the cherished
landmarks of Amsterdam and, if you

wait a while, you may see a huge barge
carefully negotiate a passage
underneath. On the opposite bank is the
bulky Koninklijk Theater Carré, built in
1887 as a circus venue, now used to
stage popular musical productions and
cabaret performances.
Retrace your steps to Keizersgracht and
walk down the left-hand embankment,
noting the variety of gable styles
represented on the buildings opposite.
Cross Utrechtsestraat and continue
along Keizersgracht, looking out for
the huge figure of Neptune on the gable
of No. 695.

6 Reguliersgracht

The next crossing marks the junction of
Keizersgracht and Reguliersgracht, at a
photogenic spot featured on countless
postcards. Five bridges span the junction
and long vistas open up in every
direction, each embankment lined by
tipsy leaning houses.
Walkers now have a choice. Continue
along the north side of Keizersgracht, and
you will pass the former Fodor Museum
(No. 609) on the right, now a modern art
gallery, and the palatial Museum van
Loon (No. 672) opposite. Alternatively,
turn right, down Reguliersgracht (named
after the Regulars, or monks, who lived
here until 1532), to return to
Rembrandtplein.

Nearby
Kerkstraat runs parallel to Keizersgracht to
the left. On the Kerkstraat/Reguliersgracht
junction there is the unusual Amstelkerk,
built in 1670 in timber as a temporary
measure – a bigger brick church was
planned but never built.

Nearly a quarter of Amsterdam's population is of non-Dutch origin, a legacy of colonialism and of the 'guest workers' policy of the 1960s. Before World War II, the Dutch Empire spanned the globe, from the Antilles and Dutch Guyana to South Africa, and from there, via the 8,000 islands of the East Indies, to Tasmania. In 1949, Indonesia was the first of the former colonies to secure independence, but ties between the two countries remain strong; thousands of Amsterdammers have island ancestry and their contribution to city life is most evident in the large number of excellent Indonesian restaurants.

Dutch Guyana – modern Surinam – gained independence in 1975 and 150,000 Surinamese have since exercised their right to settle in The Netherlands. Another 35,000 migrants from Turkey and Morocco arrived in the 1960s, deliberately imported to do the low-paid manual jobs that the Dutch themselves were not willing to do.

Amsterdammers pride themselves on a long tradition of hospitality, but tension nevertheless exists between different parts of the community. Some white residents blame incomers for crime and complain about the cost to the city of housing, welfare and unemployment benefits. Equally, immigrants blame crime on the white population, whom they see as immoral and irreligious, and they complain that their cultures are misunderstood.

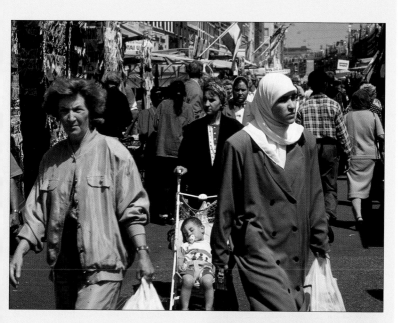

Even so, great efforts are being made to create a harmonious society. The area known as De Pijp (The Pipe) is a good example of successful integration. Most residents here are young and determined to get on.

Albert Cuypstraat, the area's colourful market (*see p138*), is a cheerful melting pot, an exotic bazaar catering to all tastes, and the best place to experience Amsterdam in all its ethnic diversity.

Images of ethnic diversity: a man of Chinese origin feeds pigeons in an open space (facing page top); Latino music at De Pijp (facing page bottom); Muslim women in headscarves in a busy street (this page above); a man of Indonesian origin selling vegetables (right)

Unknown Amsterdam: the Western Islands

If you have fallen in love with Amsterdam and want to buy a *bijou* city residence, you could do worse than head for the three man-made islands located in the western harbour. The three islands are Prinseneiland, Realeneiland and Bickerseiland, collectively known the Westelijke Eilanden (Western Islands). They were constructed in the 1630s, originally to store hazardous and inflammable materials well away from the residential heart of the city.

Elegant apartments in Prinseneiland

The stately 17th-century warehouses survive, with their huge sail-shaped window shutters. Some have already been turned into apartments, while others are in the process of being converted. Some are still used for their original purpose, storing tropical imports such as timber. Unconverted warehouses are much in demand by artists, sculptors and photographers because of their huge floor area and bohemian ambience.

As a result, the Western Islands have a distinctive 'village' atmosphere, enhanced by the lack of traffic. Herons perch on the ancient lifting bridges that link the islands, all as attractive and as well preserved as the more famous Magere Brug in the city centre. Swans, moorhens and ducks nest on the canal banks where expensive yachts are moored alongside tugs, barges and wrecked hulls – their owners intending, optimistically, to restore them one day.

The best way to reach the islands from Amsterdam Centraal Station is to walk down Haarlemmerstraat and Haarlemmerdijk, the latter a characterful street lined by inexpensive neighbourhood shops and cafés.

This is the 'real' Amsterdam, untouched by tourism, where ordinary residents shop and pass the time of day. The street ends at Haarlemmerplein where a ponderous triumphal arch, built in the 19th century as a monumental entrance to the city from Haarlem, now stands unloved on a busy traffic island.

Turn right, crossing the busy road, then pass under the railway viaduct.

Suddenly you are in a different world. Take the first bridge on the right and you will reach Prinseneiland, where the best apartments are located. Continue straight through and you will hear the sounds of hens and goats as you turn left on Bickersgracht; the source is the **Kinderboerderij de Dierencapel**, just round the bend (open: daylight hours; free admission, but donations welcome).

Carry on and you will reach Zandhoek where there is a fine row of 17th-century houses with spout, step and bell gables. Plaques on the house fronts depict Noah's Ark, St Peter and St John, anchors, boats and a white horse. The last in the row, No. 15, is a friendly restaurant, De Gouden Reael, renowned for its inexpensive regional French cuisine (*see p163*). Opposite, you will often see well-restored sailing barges moored in Westerdok.

Beyond this point the scene becomes more bleak. A lot of warehouses on Van Diemenstraat have been turned into enterprise buildings, and one, No. 410, is the Veem (Warehouse) Theatre now, where dance and mime are performed. Otherwise the empty warehouses are now being converted under the IJ-Oever Project, a hugely ambitious regeneration plan designed to provide yet more conference centres, marinas, parks and museums as well as homes for 20,000 families and office premises designed for multinational companies.

Walk all the way back to Bickersgracht and cross the canal (to the left), and you will arrive on Prinseneiland.

Many plastic artists have their studio here; there are also two galleries, one at No. 439, Maria Chailloux, and one at No. 14A, Ans Markus. Dutch buyers are more fortunate than foreign visitors – they can take out an interest-free loan from the government to buy the works on display, repaying in instalments. The idea is to encourage people of ordinary means to buy art.

Continue and soon you will emerge beneath the railway viaduct again; cross the road, walk straight on and you will find yourself back in Haarlemmerdijk.

Restored 17th-century apartments in Zandhoek

The glowing interior of the Museum Van Loon

Museum Van Loon

The atmospheric Museum Van Loon was designed in 1672 by Adriaan Dortsman and has the figures of Minerva, Mars, Vulcan and Ceres on the cornice. One of the first owners of the house was Ferdinand Bol, a pupil of Rembrandt, who married a rich wife and promptly gave up painting. Another was Catharina Trip, whose initials, along with those of her husband, Abraham van Hagen, are carved into the staircase balustrade. The house was purchased in 1884 by Hendrik van Loon and it now features a near-complete sequence of Van Loon family portraits, from 17th-century paintings to 20th-century photographs. The period furnishings all have the patina that comes from time and use, creating a mood of faded grandeur.

Keizersgracht 672. Tel: (020) 624 5255; www.museumvanloon.nl Open: Fri–Mon 11am–5pm (Jul–Aug daily). Admission charge. Trams: 16, 24 & 25. Nearby: Museum Willet-Holthuysen.

Verzetsmuseum (Dutch Resistance Museum)

The Dutch Resistance Museum is housed in a former synagogue in the wealthy Amsterdam South suburb where Anne Frank and her family lived until they went into hiding. The displays recall the many ingenious ways that the Dutch Resistance sought to sabotage the Nazi occupation.

The exhibits include a bicycle-powered printing press used for forging documents to help Jews escape arrest and for producing underground newspapers such as *Het Parool* (The Password), which continues to circulate in Amsterdam to this day.

There is a reconstruction of a hiding place used by *onderduikers*, 'divers', along with contemporary photographs, video material and radio broadcasts, all of which help to bring this fascinating subject vividly to life.

Plantage Kerlaan 61. Tel: (020) 620 2535; www.verzetsmuseum.org Open: Tue–Fri 10am–5pm, Mon, Sat–Sun & public holidays noon–5pm. Closed: 1 Jan, 30 Apr & 25 Dec. Admission charge. Trams: 6, 9, 10 & 14.

Museum Willet-Holthuysen

Of the several Golden Age houses open to the public in Amsterdam, this is the grandest. The imposing mansion was

Dutch Resistance Museum tells a story of courage and determination

built in 1689 and left to the city in 1895 along with a large collection of glass, Delftware, clocks, furniture and silver. At first nobody wanted to see a house full of 'Victorian' furniture little different to what many Amsterdammers had in their own home. The bored curator spent his time writing a scurrilous novel about the former owners and it was jokingly said that the museum was an ideal place for clandestine lovers to meet without being observed.

Visitors now come in large numbers, enjoying a glimpse below stairs of the 18th-century kitchen stacked with gleaming copper pans, before exploring the grander rooms upstairs with their ceiling paintings, Aubusson tapestries and gilded chandeliers.
Herengracht 605. Tel: (020) 523 1822; www.museumwillet-holthuysen.nl Open: Mon–Fri 10am–5pm, Sat–Sun & public holidays 11am–5pm. Closed: 1 Jan, 30 Apr & 25 Dec. Admission charge. Trams: 4, 9 & 14.

Zoo (Natura Artis Magistra)

Amsterdam's zoo opened in 1838 under the grand title of Natura Artis Magistra (Nature, Teacher of the Arts). Now known simply as Artis, the zoo offers enough attractions to fill the best part of a day. As well as 6,000 animals kept in naturalistic enclosures, there is a children's farm, a spectacular planetarium, a tropical house and a large aquarium. The ticket includes admission to two museums on the site – the Geologisch Museum illustrating the earth's evolution and the Zoologisch Museum whose tableaux and audio-visuals explain the flora and fauna of characteristic Dutch landscapes.
Plantage Kerklaan 40. Tel: (020) 523 3400; www.artis.nl Open: daily 9am–5pm, Apr–Sept until 6pm. Planetarium: closed Mon until 12.30pm. Zoologisch Museum: same hours as Artis. Admission charge. Trams: 6, 9 & 14. Nearby: Hortus Botanicus Plantage.

Animal antics at the zoo

Amsterdam has been described as a city of 'architectural good manners', a city of few ostentatious buildings but of a myriad charming details. Seventeenth-century planning laws ensured that all houses were built of brick or stone to standard widths, so that canalside homeowners had limited scope for placing their personal stamp on the property.

Still, to stand out, they varied the number and size of windows in the façade; huge expanses of gleaming glass advertised the wealth of the owner, since glass was an expensive commodity. Another way of expressing individualism was to cover the crown and sides of the gable with sculptures or ornamental frills and flourishes.

Gables were originally very plain. They were designed to disguise the roof ridge, built at right angles to the canal. The earliest type was the point gable, a simple inverted 'V' that precisely followed the shape of the roof timbers.

Next came the spout gable which is the same as a point gable except with a chimney-like rectangular protusion from the point; these two types are commonly seen on the earliest surviving warehouses. By 1600, the more ornate step gable was in use for domestic buildings and it remained in vogue until Philips Vingboons designed the first neck gable, shaped like the shoulders and neck of a wine bottle, for the Cromhouthuisen

ANNO 1739

(now the Bijbels Museum) in 1638. This quickly became fashionable, and was joined by the bell gable in 1660.

From 1670, the owners of grand houses on the Golden Bend of the canal circle began to reject the traditional Dutch style. Sandstone was used for the façades instead of brick and the frontages were now too wide to be spanned by a single gable. Instead the roof line was hidden by pediments, balustrades and cornices, often embellished with Baroque swags and garlands or Neo-Classical sculpture. However, right up to the present century, the gable remained in use for humbler homes and a short stroll along the canal circle reveals just how well these simple geometric shapes lend themselves to an infinite number of variations.

Look up and feast your eyes on gable art. In the face of conformity in matters architectural, decorative gables express Amsterdam individuality

Walk: Nieuwmarkt and the University Quarter

This walk covers some important but little-visited architectural monuments in the south of the old city. *Allow 1½ hours.*

Start at Dam Square and walk to the right of the Nationaal Monument, down Damstraat. Continue past the interesting shop windows of Oude Doelenstraat into Oude Hoogstraat.

1 Oost-Indisch Huis

A low arch beside No. 24 leads into the courtyard of East India House, the former headquarters of the once-powerful trading company dating from 1659.

Return to Oude Hoogstraat, turning right, then left on to Kloveniersburgwal.

2 Trippenhuis

On the opposite bank is the palatial Trippenhuis, built between 1660 and 1664 by Justus Vingboons for the Trip brothers, who made their fortune in the armaments trade. The interior (not open to the public) housed the Rijksmuseum collection during most of the 19th century. On this side of the canal is the Kleine (Little) Trippenhuis, which is also known as the House of Mr Trip's Coachman. It dates from 1696 and the frontage is only 4m wide – the modest coachman, so the popular story goes, said he would be happy with a house as wide as his employer's front door.

Take the next turning left, Koestraat.

3 Wijnkopersgildehuis

Halfway down, at No. 10, is the former headquarters of the wine importers' guild, a building dating from 1633. The frieze above the door depicts St Urban standing among grape vines.

Return to Kloveniersburgwal and turn left up to Nieuwmarkt.

4 Nieuwmarkt

This vast empty square still has a few stalls to remind us that it was once a major market. The dominant building is the Waag (Weighhouse), originally built in 1488 as a gate in the city wall. In 1617, it was fitted out with scales for weighing naval anchors and cannon. The octagonal tower in the centre, added in 1690, served as the Theatricum Anatomicum, the lecture theatre of the Surgeons' Guild (as depicted in Rembrandt's *The Anatomy Lecture of Dr Jan Deyman*). The Waag now houses changing exhibitions and a restaurant.
Walk down the opposite bank of Kloveniersburgwal for a closer look at the Trippenhuis. Note the two doors, one for each of the Trip brothers; behind the unified façade there were two separate residences – the middle windows are dummies, masking the dividing wall. Turn left in Nieuwe Hoogstraat and first right in Zanddwarsstraat.

5 Zuiderkerk

Straight ahead is the soaring tower of Zuiderkerk (South Church). The church, designed in 1603 by Hendrik de Keyser, was the first in the city to be built specifically for Calvinist worship.
Walk to Raamgracht and, after walking three sides of a square, continue down Groenburgwal, turning right at the timber lifting bridge.

6 Staalstraat

This short but picturesque street is lined with up-market antique shops. The Saaihal (Serge Hall), No. 7, was built in 1614 by Pieter de Keyser for the clothworkers' guild.

Cross the iron lifting bridge, turn right on Kloveniersburgwal and look for a gate on the left just after No. 82.

7 Oudemanhuispoort

Above the 'Gate of the Old Men's Home', sculptures show Charity between two beggars. On the right is the former old people's home, built in 1786, now part of the university, founded in 1876.
Walk through the passage.

8 Huis aan de Drie Grachten

Facing you as you emerge is the delightful House on the Three Canals, built in 1609, and so called because it has three step-gabled façades, each looking out on to a different canal.
Walk past the house and turn right up OZ Voorburgwal.

9 Agnietenkapel

This former chapel, at No. 231, was the first home of the Atheneum Illustre, a learned society and forerunner of the University of Amsterdam. It now houses the University Museum with exhibits from the University Historical Collection.
Further up on the right, look for No. 197, an Art Deco brick gateway.

10 Grand Amsterdam Hotel

Through the gateway to the right is the Grand Amsterdam hotel, the former Town Hall, built in 1647 as the Admiralty headquarters. It became the Town Hall in 1808 when Louis Napoleon turned the original Stadhuis, on Dam Square, into his royal palace.
Take the next turn left, Oude Doelenstraat, to return to Dam Square.

Amsterdam Environs

Travel within The Netherlands is extremely easy thanks to an excellent integrated public transport system. Many of the sites covered in this section are accessible by fast, cheap and reliable InterCity trains which depart from Amsterdam Centraal Station every 15 or 30 minutes. Journey times are short: Haarlem is only 13 minutes away, Utrecht 28 minutes, Den Haag (The Hague) 35 minutes and Rotterdam an hour. Amsterdam, therefore, makes a perfect base for exploring the wider attractions of The Netherlands. All-inclusive day-trip tickets (Rail Idee, or 'Rail Idea') offer the cheapest way to travel; they include the cost of the rail fare and admission at a discount to almost all attractions. The Rail Idee can be purchased separately if you already have a valid entrance ticket or pass.

Alternatively you can buy a one-day travel pass which allows unlimited use of the transport network. Details of both are given in the useful *Exploring Holland by Train* booklet which is available from the information centre in Amsterdam Centraal Station or before you go from The Netherlands Board of Tourism offices.

Some destinations close to Amsterdam are not on the rail network

Harbour view of Rotterdam, chief port of The Netherlands

Amsterdam Environs

but are easily reached by buses that go from the main terminus outside Amsterdam Centraal Station, or the suburban station, Amsterdam Amstel.

If you prefer to have everything organised for you, there are numerous coach tours covering the same destination. These can be booked in person at the VVV Informatiekantoor (Tourist Information Office) at Stationsplein 10, in Amsterdam. Once you arrive at your destination you can obtain free maps and leaflets from the excellent VVV Tourist Information Offices which are usually located on the main square or near the station. You can also hire a bike for the day at most stations by presenting some form of identification and paying a small deposit.

Aalsmeer

The Aalsmeer Flower Auction
(Verenigde Bloemenveiling Aalsmeer,
or VBA) is the biggest commercial
flower market in the world. It is well
worth visiting if you are fond of plants
or just enjoy the bustle of a busy
commercial market. You do have to be
an early riser, however, to catch the
action: the auctions are at their busiest
around 9am, especially on Mondays.

Visitors watch the proceedings from
an elevated gallery which provides a
bird's-eye view of the auction itself and
all the sorting and despatch work that
goes on behind the scenes. Recorded
commentaries, in seven languages,
explain what is going on.

The VBA, founded in 1968, is a cooperative venture with a membership of
5,000 growers who sell their pot plants
and cut flowers at Aalsmeer, paying a
commission of 5 per cent of sales to
fund the operation. Sales are conducted
using the 'Dutch auction' system. This
works in a way that is the opposite of
normal auction procedure, with prices
starting at the top and coming down
until a buyer is found. Prices are
indicated by a huge clock above the
auctioneer's head marked out in
divisions from 100 down to 1. The clock
pointer starts at 100 – the highest price
– and sweeps downwards until a buyer,
seated at a computerised desk, presses a
button to stop the clock at the price he
or she is prepared to pay.

Computerisation is the key to the
speed and efficiency of the whole
operation. Invoices and dispatch
information are prepared automatically
as soon as the 'buy' button is pressed.

An auction of colours at Aalsmeer

The computer also handles all the
currency calculations – more than 80
per cent of the produce sold here is
exported.

Some 10,000 transactions an hour are
conducted in this way in five separate
auction rooms devoted to different types
of plants. The lots are delivered to the
buyer within 15 minutes of the sale;
around 350 buyers rent packing space
on the premises and some 2,000 trucks,
laden with sweet-smelling produce, leave
the building daily for all parts of Europe.

The market is huge; with an area
equivalent to 100 football pitches
(715,000sq m), it is said to be the biggest
commercial building in the world.
Market staff use bicycles to get around.
Aalsmeer is big business in every way;
The Netherlands is the world's leading
producer of pot plants and flowers, with
51 per cent of the market, and much of
that produce passes through here.

On the lighter side: once a year, on the
first Saturday of September, everyone
involved in the market – growers,

buyers and florists – stages a huge and colourful parade of imaginatively decorated cars and trucks smothered beneath a massive tapestry of flowers, from Aalsmeer to the centre of Amsterdam.

12km southwest of Amsterdam at Legmeerdijk 313, Aalsmeer. Tel: (0297) 392 185. Getting there: bus 172 from Amsterdam Centraal Station. Open: Mon–Fri 7.30–11am. Admission charge.

Alkmaar

Alkmaar is famed for the traditional cheese market held in the main square every Friday morning in summer months. White-garbed porters in straw hats (red, green, blue or yellow, denoting the particular group to which they belong) carry the huge rounds of yellow-waxed cheese on wooden sledges across the square into the Renaissance **Waaggebouw** (Weigh House) where the actual selling takes place. The streets around the square are crammed with stalls selling antiques, crafts and – of course – local cheese. Barrel organs and buskers add to the festive atmosphere. The town itself has several fine buildings: the 15th-century **Grote Kerk** (Great Church), the **Stadhuis** (Town Hall) of 1520 and the Waaggebouw of 1582 (housing a cheese museum) can all be visited. The **Stedelijk Museum** has an interesting collection of antique toys.

37km northwest of Amsterdam. Getting there: train line 1 to Den Helder. Journey time 32 minutes. Tourist information: Waagplein 2–3. Tel: (072) 511 4284; www.vvvweb.nl Cheese market open: mid-Apr–mid-Sept, Fri 10am–12.30pm.

Say cheese at Alkmaar

Windmills at the open-air Arnhem Museum

Arnhem

The name of Arnhem will always be associated with Operation Market Garden, the heroic but disastrous World War II battle which was immortalised in the film, *A Bridge Too Far*. The battle was an ambitious attempt to end the war in time for Christmas 1944. The military leaders involved, Field Marshal Montgomery and General Eisenhower, planned to invade Germany after capturing the strategic Rhine bridge at Arnhem. This involved flying troops into the heart of The Netherlands, still under Nazi occupation. General Browning, in charge of the Airborne Divisions, had misgivings about the operation, and it was he who told Montgomery, 'We might be going a bridge too far'.

He was right; when 35,000 troops were parachuted into Arnhem on 17 September 1944 they found the bridges heavily defended by the tanks and artillery of the 2nd SS Panzer Division. Some 600 Allied troops fought their way to Arnhem bridge and defended it for four days before being forced to

withdraw. The battle ended with defeat for the Allies and the death of thousands of soldiers.

Visitors can visit the battle sites and trace the course of events, by means of models and an audio-visual presentation, at the **Airborne Museum** in Oosterbeek, 8km west of Arnhem. Nearby, on the north bank of the Rhine, in Oosterbeek is the **Airborne War Cemetery**, beautifully maintained by the War Graves Commission.

Arnhem has two other outstanding attractions. On the outskirts of the town is the **Nederlands Openlucht** (Open-Air) **Museum** where 80 traditional buildings have been rescued from their original sites and reconstructed. These include windmills, farmhouses, schools, factories, shops, churches and inns dating from the 17th century. The interiors are used to display traditional costumes, folk art, furniture and tools, and there are regular craft demonstrations.

Some 6km to the north of Arnhem is the **Nationaal Park Hoge Veluwe**, a huge tract of forest and heath. Free bikes provide the means of getting around and the main highlight is the **Kröller-Müller Museum**, at the centre of the park, where over 200 works by Van Gogh are displayed, together with works by Picasso, Braque and many modern artists. In the sculpture garden around the museum, works by Henry Moore, Rodin, Barbara Hepworth and others are all the more entrancing for their background of trees, water and open skies.

72km southeast of Amsterdam. Getting there: train lines 4 & 5 to Nijmegen;

*journey time 75 minutes; change at
Arnhem for Oosterbeek, journey time
4 minutes. Bus 3 (to Alteveer) goes from
Arnhem station to the Openluchtmuseum,
and bus 107 (to Harderwijk) goes to the
Park Hoge Veluwe; in summer a special
museum bus, No. 12, serves both museums.
Tourist information: Stationsplein 45.
Tel: (0900) 202 4075.*
*Airborne Museum open: Mon–Sat
10am–5pm, Sun & public holidays
noon–5pm. Openlucht Museum
open: mid-Apr–Oct, daily 10am–5pm.
Admission charge. Hoge Veluwe Park
visitors' centre open: daily 8am–sunset.
Kröller-Müller Museum open: Tue–Sat
10am–5pm (sculpture garden closes
4.30pm).*

Aviodome (Netherlands National Aerospace Museum)

A short train ride from Schiphol is
Lelystad, where you can find the Dutch
National Aviation Theme Park and
Museum. It is popular with children,
who are allowed to climb into the
cockpit of one of the aircraft. The
dome-shaped building shelters various
historic aircraft, ranging from the
Wright Flyer of 1903 to a Mercury space
capsule. It also celebrates the Dutch
contribution to aviation history; the
Dutch national carrier, KLM, was the
world's first commercial airline, flying
locally built Fokker FVII aircraft from
1919. Posters and KLM memorabilia of
the 1920s evoke the romance of flight in
those early days.

There is a sober reminder of the aerial
warfare of World War II in the salvaged
remains of a British bomber, and plenty
of diversions in the form of films, slide
shows and an exhibition on the
importance of Schiphol airport to the
Dutch economy.
Pelikaan 50, Lelystad Airport.
*Getting there: train to Schiphol station
then train from platform 2 for Lelystad.
Take bus 148 to Lelystad Airport, from
where the Aviodome is signposted.*
Tel: (320) 289 840; www.aviodome.nl
*Open: Tue–Sun 10am–5pm and Mon
during school holidays. Closed: 1 Jan.
Admission charge.*

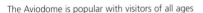
The Aviodome is popular with visitors of all ages

Delft

Delft has given its name to the distinctive blue-and-white pottery that has been produced here since the 17th century when Dutch East India Company ships first started bringing back delicate porcelain wares from China. The potters of the region immediately began to copy these wares but decorated their plates, jugs, tiles and tulip jars with scenes from everyday life, biblical

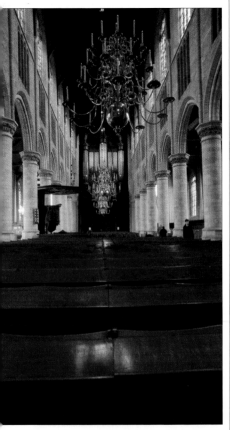

The 15th-century Nieuwe Kerk in Delft

subjects and Dutch landscapes. The industry nearly collapsed in the 19th century in the face of competition from England. The only firm to survive in Delft was **De Porceleyne Fles**, founded in 1653 and still going strong. If you want to know more you should head straight for this company's Visitor Centre, which exhibits typical products and offers factory tours throughout the day.

There is, though, far more to Delft than pottery. On the main square, Markt, you will find the Renaissance **Stadhuis** (Town Hall) built in 1618 by Hendrik de Keyser. The statue in the centre of the square commemorates the lawyer Hugo Grotius, born in Delft in 1583, whose great work on the conduct of war laid the foundations for modern international law.

Opposite, **Nieuwe Kerk**, with its soaring 15th-century choir, contains the mausoleum of William of Orange, leader of the Dutch revolt against Spanish rule and the father of The Netherlands. The monument, another work by Hendrik de Keyser, was designed in 1614; in allegorical form, it depicts the ideals on which the newly independent Dutch Republic was based – liberty, justice, religion and fortitude.

William of Orange met an untimely end in Delft in 1584; he was assassinated in the nearby convent of St Agatha, now the **Prinsenhof Museum**, which William used as his campaign headquarters during the war against Spain. The bullet holes made by his assassin (Balthazar Gerards, a fanatical Catholic and a supporter of Spanish rule) can be seen behind glass in room 8, the Moordzaal (Murder Hall).

Apart from this morbid memorial, the rest of the museum is a delight. The traceried Gothic windows of the 15th-century convent look out on to attractive courtyard gardens and the walls are hung with paintings by artists of the Delft School.

Opposite the museum is the 14th-century **Oude Kerk**, with its leaning tower and beautiful 16th-century transept, built in the style known, appropriately, as Flamboyant Gothic. Inside there are the tombs of Vermeer and the Delft-born inventor of the microscope, Antonie van Leeuwenhoek, along with memorials to the Admirals Piet Hein and Maarten Tromp; the latter's tomb is carved with a realistic battle scene praised by Samuel Pepys as 'a sea-fight cut in marble, the smoke the best expressed that ever I saw'.

From the church it is worth walking the length of Oude Delft, a leafy canal lined by elegant houses. At No. 199, the best collection of antique Delftware in the city can be found, housed in the **Museum Lambert van Meerten**; the interior is covered in tiles, ranging from large-scale battle scenes to cheerful depictions of children's games.

At the opposite end of Oude Delft, the courtyard houses at No. 39 once served as an office of the VOC (Verenigde Oostindische Companie, better known as the Dutch East India Company). Opposite the huge former arsenal, the Armamentarium, is now the **Nederlands Legermuseum** (Dutch Army Museum).

58km southwest of Amsterdam.

Tempting displays of Delft

Rotterdam CS. Getting there: train journey time 55 minutes.
Tourist information: Hippolytusbuurt 4.
Tel: (0900) 515 1555; www.delft.nl

Delft
De Porceleyne Fles
Rotterdamseweg 196. Tel: (015) 251 2030; www.royaldelft.com. Open: Mon–Sat 9am–5pm, Apr–Oct also Sun 9.30am–5pm. Admission charge.
Museum Lambert van Meerten
Oude Delft 199. Tel: (015) 260 2199. Open: Tue–Sat 10am–5pm, Sun & public holidays 1–5pm. Admission charge.
Nederlands Legermuseum
Korte Geer 1. Tel: (015) 215 0500; www.legermuseum.nl. Open: Mon–Fri 10am–5pm, Sat–Sun noon–5pm. Admission charge.
Nieuwe Kerk
Markt. Tel: (015) 212 3025. Open: Apr–Oct, Mon–Sat 9am–6pm; Nov–Mar, Mon–Sat 11am–4pm. Admission charge.
Oude Kerk
Oude Delft. Tel: (015) 212 3015. Open: Mon–Sat 10am–5pm. Admission charge.
Museum het Prinsenhof
St Agathaplein 1. Tel: (015) 260 2358. Open: Tue–Sat 10am–5pm, Sun & public holidays 1–5pm. Admission charge.

Edam

Edam competes with Gouda for the title of cheese capital of The Netherlands; in terms of quantity of output Edam wins but, in contrast to Gouda, Edam has not turned its cheese industry into a major tourist attraction. Instead, the town is noted for the quiet calm of its numerous waterways and wooden bridges, though visitors can buy the familiar round balls of soft cheese, wrapped in a protective skin of red or yellow wax, at the ancient **Kaasmarkt** (Cheese Market) on Waagplein, built in 1592.

The delightful **Edams Museum** on Damplein occupies a late Gothic house of 1530 whose small dark rooms, ladder-like stairs and hidden cupboard beds are reminiscent of life on board a ship. The building even has a curious floating cellar which sways as you walk across the floor – built, according to the local story, by a retired ship's captain who was nostalgic for the feel of the sea. Equally eccentric are the museum's portraits of three local characters, one extremely fat, another very tall and the third, Pieter Langebaard, who had, true to his name, a very long beard which he showed off as he toured The Netherlands to raise funds for the local orphanage. The town's other important monument is the **Grote Kerk** (Great Church), rebuilt after a fire in 1602 and notable for its stained glass of 1606 depicting trademarks and historical scenes. Several operators offer boat tours in summer from Edam to neighbouring towns around the former Zuider Zee.

22km north of Amsterdam.
Getting there: bus 112, 114 & 116 from Amsterdam Centraal Station; journey time 35 minutes.
Tourist information: Damplein 1.
Tel: (0299) 315 125; www.vvv-edam.nl
Kaasmarkt open: Jul–Aug, Wed 10.30am–12.30pm. Edams Museum open: Easter–autumn half-term school holiday, Tue–Sat 10am–4.30pm, Sun 1.30–4.30pm. Admission charge.

Edam, where the local cheese is on offer

The stained-glass window at Gouda is part of a series of windows at St Janskerk

Gouda

For those interested in the traditional cheese market, Gouda should be visited on Thursday mornings in summer. Here white-coated experts handle and sample the cheese with all the respect usually reserved for the finest wines. Gouda develops different characteristics as it ages and several types are sold: *jong* (young) is creamy and mild, *belegen* is firmer and has matured for four months, *oud* (old) is 10 months old and *overjarig*, the most expensive, is at least a year old, and should be pungent and crumbly. In addition there are cumin (*komijn*) and clove (*kruidnegel*) flavoured varieties.

The market takes place against the backdrop of the fine Flemish-style Stadhuis, built in 1450 and decorated with statues of Burgundian counts and countesses, a reminder that this part of The Netherlands was under Burgundian rule in the 15th century.

The medieval quarter, with its quiet cobbled lanes, lies to the south of the Markt. St Janskerk has the best stained glass in The Netherlands, a magnificent series of windows given by various donors when the church was rebuilt after a fire in 1522. Local guilds were among the sponsors and they chose appropriate biblical themes – *Jonah and the Whale* for the fishmongers, *Balaam and his Ass* for the butchers. Philip II of Spain donated *The Last Supper* and he is depicted with his wife, Queen Mary I of England. William the Silent, who was shortly to lead the Dutch revolt against Philip II's rule, donated *Christ Driving the Money Changers from the Temple*.

Opposite the church is the **Catharina Gasthuis**, founded as a hospice for travellers in the 14th century, now housing a fine collection of medieval art and Impressionist paintings by members of The Hague School. The town's other museum, **De Moriaan** (The Moor) is a beautifully preserved 17th-century tobacco shop displaying a collection of clay pipes, located on the former harbour at Westhaven 29.

52km south of Amsterdam.
Getting there: train to Utrecht then change for train to Rotterdam CS/Don Haeg CS. Journey time 50 minutes.
Tourist information: Markt 27.
Tel: (0900) 4683 2888; www.vvvgouda.nl
Cheese market open: mid-Jun–mid-Aug, Thur 10am–12.30pm. Stadhuis open: Mon–Fri 9am–noon & 2–4pm, Sat 11am–3pm. St Janskerk open: Apr–Oct, Mon–Sat 9am–5pm; Nov–Mar, Mon–Sat 10am–4pm. Catharina Gasthuis open: Mon–Sat 10am–5pm, Sun noon–5pm. De Moriaan open: same as Catharina Gasthuis.

Mauritshuis Museum at Den Haag

Den Haag (The Hague)

After Amsterdam, Den Haag has more
to offer than any other city in The
Netherlands and the museums alone
will occupy more than a day, so it is
worth considering an overnight stay.
Den Haag is an abbreviated form of the
city's old name, 's Gravenhaage,
meaning the Count's Hedge. This hedge
surrounded the hunting lodge of the
medieval Counts of Holland, later
rebuilt as a castle. The town grew up
around the castle and its future was
assured when Den Haag became the
political capital of The Netherlands in
1586, chosen because it offered a neutral
meeting ground for the leaders of the
seven independent provinces created
under the Treaty of Utrecht after the
Spanish had been driven out.

The former castle of the Counts of
Holland, the 13th-century Ridderzaal,
still stands at the heart of the city. It is
surrounded by the buildings of the
Dutch Parliament on one side and by
the **Mauritshuis** on the other, a graceful
building whose façade is reflected in the
Hof Vijver lake, all that remains of the
original castle moat. The Mauritshuis
museum contains several important
works: Rogier van de Weyden's
Lamentation, Rembrandt's *The Anatomy
Lesson of Dr Nicolaes Tulp*, his first
public commission, the charming
Goldfinch, by Rembrandt's gifted pupil,
Fabritius, and Vermeer's *View of Delft*.
Andy Warhol's *Queen Beatrix* brings the
collection up to date.

The Mauritshuis is only one of several
museums surrounding the Hof Vijver;
on a short stroll you can sample the
popular **Museum Gevangenpoort**, once
a prison and now a 'torture museum', or
the **Galerij Prins Willem V** (Buitenhof
35), a small gallery crammed with Old
Masters. The **Haags Historisch Museum**
(Korte Vijverberg 7) displays old
paintings of the city.

If shopping appeals more than
museums, head for **The Passage**, off
Buitenhof, an elegant 19th-century
arcade leading to the pedestrianised
shopping streets around the 15th-
century **Oude Kerk**. Noordeindestraat is
definitely for the wealthy, with its
couturiers, antique dealers and
restaurants patronised by diplomats.

Continuing up this street, past the
royal Paleis Noordeinde, you will reach
the *Panorama Mesdag*, an intriguing
relic of the 19th century, and a fine
example of *trompe l'oeil* painting. The
circular canvas, 120m long, shows an
extraordinarily realistic view of the

nearby coastal resort of Scheveningen as it was in 1881. More works by Hendrik Mesdag, a leading Impressionist painter of The Hague School, can be seen at the artist's former home, now the Museum Mesdag, at Laan van Meerdevoort 7.

Just to the north is the huge **Vredespaleis** (Peace Palace) founded after The Hague Peace Conference of 1899 and financed by the Scottish-born American millionaire Andrew Carnegie. The aim was to provide a forum for resolving international disputes – a worthy aim, though it did not prevent two world wars. Now it is the seat of the International Court of Justice.

Beyond this point is the best of the city's museums, the **Haags Gemeentemuseum**. This has a big collection of modern art from The Hague School to Mondriaan, Delftware, musical instruments and historic costume.

The **Omniversum planetarium** next door appeals to children, as does the **Madurodam** miniature town at George Maduroplein 1, on the road to Scheveningen: this is a fascinating 1:25 scale reproduction of Dutch landscape features – towns, farms, the port of Rotterdam and Schiphol airport.

Scheveningen itself, almost a suburb of Den Haag, is a breezy North Sea coastal resort. Its attractions include an imposing Empire-style hotel, called the Kurhaus, a model of Jules Verne's *Nautilus* submarine, the Holland Casino, good fish restaurants and a long stretch of clean sandy beach.

60km southwest of Amsterdam.
Getting there: train to Den Haag HS (Hollands Spoor) station, then change for Den Haag CS (Centraal Station).

Journey time 55 minutes.
Tourist information: Koningin Julianaplein 30, to the right of the station exit. Tel: (0900) 340 3505; www.denhaag.com

Galerij Prins Willem
Buitenhof 35. Tel: (070) 302 3456. Open: Tue–Sun 11am–4pm. Admission charge.

Haags Gemeentemuseum
Stadhouderslaan 41. Tel: (070) 338 1111; www.gemeentemuseum.nl. Open: Tue–Sun 11am–5pm. Admission charge.

Madurodam
George Maduroplein 1. Tel: (070) 355 3900; www.madurodam.nl. Open: daily, late Mar–Jun 9am–8pm, Jul–Aug 9am–10pm, Sept–late Mar 9am–6pm. Admission charge.

Mauritshuis
Korte Vijverberg 8. Tel: (070) 302 3456; www.mauritshuis.nl. Open: Tue–Sat 10am–5pm, Sun & public holidays 11am–5pm (also open Mon in summer). Admission charge.

Museum Gevangenpoort
Buitenhof 33. Tel: (070) 346 0861; www.gevangenpoort.nl. Open: Tue–Fri 11am–4pm, Sat–Sun noon–4pm. Admission charge.

Museum Mesdag
Laan van Meerdervoort 7f. Tel: (070) 362 1434; www.museummesdag.nl. Open: Tue–Sun noon–5pm. Admission charge.

Omniversum
President Kennedylaan 5. Tel: (0900) 666 4837; www.omniversum.nl. Open: daily during school holidays 10am–10pm, otherwise Mon 9.30am–3pm, Tue–Wed 9.30am–5pm, Thur–Fri 9.30am–10pm, Sat–Sun 10am–10pm; planetarium performances on the hour. Admission charge.

Panorama Mesdag
Zeestraat 65. Tel: (070) 364 4544; www.mesdag.nl. Open: Mon–Sat 10am–5pm, Sun & public holidays noon–5pm. Admission charge.

Ridderzaal
Binnenhof 8A. Tel: (070) 364 6144. Open: guided tours Mon–Sat 10am–4pm. Admission charge.

Den Haag is the home of the Dutch royal family and several operators offer 'royal tours' taking in the lovely 17th-century Huis ten Bosch (House in the Woods – not open to the public), where Queen Beatrix lives amid extensive parkland to the east of the city.

Wilhelmina Armgard Beatrix acceded to the throne following the abdication of her mother Queen Juliana. Her coronation as Queen Beatrix on 30 April 1980 caused great controversy. The planned festivities turned into a full-scale riot as protestors, objecting to the cost of the investiture and seeking to highlight the housing crisis, fought with police in Amsterdam. Since then Queen Beatrix has worked hard to sweep away the mystique of the monarchy. Though she is the second richest woman in Europe (after Queen Elizabeth II of Britain) she avoids ostentation, loves cycling in the countryside and has often said she would have been a social worker if she had not been queen. Her husband Prince Claus, a former West German diplomat, once suffered from depression and won praise for talking about it publicly and for giving help to others with a similar problem. By behaving like an ordinary modern family, the Dutch royals have overcome any lingering resentment about their privileged position.

Queen Beatrix also works with consummate professionalism to promote Dutch interests at home and abroad. Once asked to define her job she replied; 'The kingdom is something to be marketed, just like oranges,' a humorous, if unintentional, reference to the fact that she is descended from the French House of Orange.

She has three sons, and the eldest, Prins Willem Alexander Claus George Ferdinand, born in 1967, is the first male heir to the Dutch crown in over

a hundred years. On 2 February 2002, Prince Willem Alexander married Maxime Zorreguieta, an Argentinian from the higher middle class, whose looks and appearance charmed many. The royal family has the respect and affection of the general public – as can be seen when the whole country joins in the annual celebrations on 30 April in honour of Koninginnedag, the Queen's official birthday.

Opposite: The Royal Palace in Amsterdam, occasional residence of Queen Beatrix; above: everyone enjoys the Queen's Day on 30 April, from state dignitaries to the rest of the nation

Haarlem

Haarlem, the capital of Noord Holland province, is a mere 13 minutes from Amsterdam by train but a world away in atmosphere. Compared with the bustle of Amsterdam, Haarlem has a peaceful, almost rural, atmosphere, and it is a pleasure to wander through its quiet streets or along the banks of the River Spaarne which winds its way round the historic centre of the city.

On arrival, the station itself is worth more than a passing glance; built in 1908, it is a stylish building of Art Nouveau tilework, honey-coloured woodwork and cast iron. Jansweg leads from the station to the magnificent

The ornate interior of Grote Kerk

Grote Kerk, begun in the 14th century and completed in the 16th. The church was a favourite subject of 17th-century painters and may already be familiar from pictures in Amsterdam's Rijksmuseum. The simple white-painted interior serves to highlight the mighty Christian Müller organ, one of the largest in the world, and its Baroque ornamentation. Mozart (aged 10), Liszt, and Saint-Saëns have all played at its keyboard and there are regular recitals during the week. Many small shops cluster around the church walls; the one on the north side was built in 1603 as the **Vishal** (Fish Market). Alongside is the city's main square, **Grote Markt**, surrounded by notable buildings: the Renaissance **Stadhuis**, the **Vleeshal** (Meat Market) of 1603 with its giant ox-head carvings, and the **Hoofdwacht** (Guardhouse) of 1650. The statue by the church is of LJ Coster to whom the Dutch attribute the invention of printing.

To the east of Grote Kerk, Damstraat leads past the **Waag** (Weighhouse) of 1598 to the River Spaarne and its pretty white bridge. Alongside is the **Teylers Museum**, founded in 1778, and preserved in its original state. The Netherlands' oldest museum, it is full of beautifully crafted scientific instruments of polished wood and brass and cases of fossils. Also on display is a collection of drawings, including works by Michelangelo, Rembrandt and Raphael.

Returning to Grote Markt, head south down Warmoesstraat, Schagchelstraat and Groot Heiligland to the city's main attraction, the **Frans Halsmuseum**. This is located in the Oude Mannenhuis, formerly a home for elderly men, built in 1608. Frans Hals was born in Antwerp but settled in Haarlem in the 1580s and, despite being one of the greatest portrait artists of his age, ended up an impoverished inmate of this same institution.

The museum has eight of the artist's large group paintings, including one of the governors of the home, painted when Frans Hals was over 80 but quite evidently still in full possession of his powers: the picture expresses something of the bitterness he must have felt as the recipient of charity from these stern-faced and reproachful burghers. Van Gogh admired the outstanding use of colour, counting no less than 27 different tones of black.

Another superbly realised picture shows the members of the Civic Guard of St Adrian at their annual banquet, flush-faced and evidently well into their cups. Their inebriated state is conveyed partly by the unflattering facial expressions but also by the way that Frans Hals has presented the ruffs, beards and ceremonial sashes at all sorts of tipsy angles – looking at the picture too long will make your own head begin to spin. From the museum you can weave your way back to the Grote Markt through streets where time seems to have stood still and where several shops retain their original 18th- or 19th-century fittings. Kerkstraat has a particularly good concentration of antique shops leading up to the 17th-century **Nieuwekerk**. From here, either take Lange Annastraat north to see the 17th-century *hofjes* (almshouses) that line either side, or walk

Haarlem's Frans Halsmuseum

back up the main shopping street, Grote Houtstraat. In Grote Markt you can rest your feet at one of several popular pavement cafés, and there are more characterful shops on Kruisstraat, leading back to the station.

23km west of Amsterdam.
Getting there: train to Hamlem/Den Haag/Zandroort; journey time 15 minutes. Tourist information: Stationsplein 1. Tel: (0900) 616 1600.

Frans Halsmuseum
Groot Heiligland 62. Tel: (023) 511 5775; www.franshalsmuseum.nl. Open: Mon–Sat 11am–5pm, Sun & public holidays noon–5pm. Closed 1 Jan & 25 Dec. Admission charge.
Grote Kerk
Oude Groenmarkt 23. Tel: (023) 553 2040. Open: Mon–Sat 10am–4pm; guided tours Sat. Free admission.
Teylers Museum
Spaarne 16. Tel: (023) 531 9010; www.teylersmuseum.nl. Open: Tue–Sat 10am–5pm, Sun & public holidays noon–5pm. Closed: Mon, 1 Jan & 25 Dec. Admission charge.

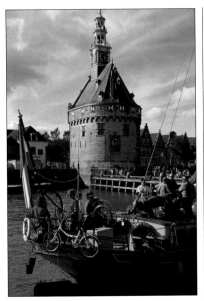
The unique charm of Hoorn

Hoorn

Hoorn was a major port until it was cut off from the sea by the damming of the Zuider Zee (IJsselmeer). Several famous mariners were born here. JP Coen, whose statue is in the main square, founded the colony of Batavia (today's Jakarta, the capital of Indonesia), Willem Schouten rounded the southern tip of the Americas in 1616 and named it Kap Hoorn (Cape Horn) after his native town, and Abel Tasman sailed from here to discover Tasmania and New Zealand.

The historic harbour quarter from where all these momentous voyages began is well preserved and lined with old warehouses. EV Lucas, the English travel writer, described the town in 1905 as 'rising from the sea like an enchanted city … its spires and harbour tower beautifully unreal'. That same view can be enjoyed in summer by taking a boat excursion into the IJsselmeer from the pier in front of the harbour tower, the Hoofdtoren, built in 1532, and given its spire in 1651.

In the town centre, the main attraction is the **Westfries Museum** (Rode Steen 1). This occupies an ornate Mannerist building of 1632, built when Hoorn was capital of the now defunct West Friesland province and decorated with the coats of arms of the region's principal towns. The interiors evoke the splendours of the Golden Age with their 17th-century furnishings, costumes, toys and reconstructed shops. Rode Steen is also the venue for a craft fair every Wednesday in July and August at which costumed stallholders demonstrate traditional crafts such as lacemaking and clog carving.

37km north of Amsterdam.
Getting there: train line to Enkhuizen; journey time 37 minutes.
Tourist information: Veemarkt 4.
Tel: (072) 511 4284; www.vvvweb.nl
Westfries Museum (www.wfm.nl). Open: Mon–Fri 11am–5pm, Sat, Sun & public holidays 2–5pm (Apr–Sept, Sun noon–5pm).

Keukenhof and Lisse

Keukenhof (Stationsweg 166A) is the showcase of the Dutch bulb industry, a 32-ha park which erupts into riotous colour every year from late March to late May. This spectacle, described as 'the greatest flower show on earth', attracts half a million visitors but the park is big enough to accommodate them all (not so the cafés, however, which get crowded – wise visitors bring a picnic with them).

The wooded park is threaded by a 16-km network of paths and the potentially garish effect of millions of bulbs is mitigated by skilful planting; variety is provided by the soft green of the woodland putting out new leaves early in the season, followed by the snowy blossoms of Japanese cherry trees and, later in the year, by masses of azalea and rhododendron blooms. The peak of the season occurs at the end of April when there is a huge flower parade on the streets of the nearby town of Lisse.

Keukenhof is located in the heart of the *bloembollenstreek*, the bulb-growing strip, which stretches from Haarlem south to Leiden. This compact area can be explored by bicycle from Leiden, Haarlem or Lisse using maps available from VVV Tourist Information Offices. The cycleways are well marked but can be crowded, especially at weekends. The bulbfields are a spectacular but shortlived sight; commercial growers allow the bulbs to flower just long enough to check that they are true to colour and free from virus and disease. The flowers are then picked, or even mown off, so that the bulb uses its energies in growing new bulbs rather than seed.

The fascinating history of bulb culture in The Netherlands is covered by the **Museum de Zwarte Tulp** (Museum of the Black Tulip) in Lisse (Grachtweg 2A). Here visitors can learn about modern hi-tech production techniques and about the tulip mania that gripped the country after the first bulbs began to

be imported from Turkey from 1630; speculation in rare varieties led to massive fortunes being won and lost.

32km southwest of Amsterdam. Getting there: operators compete to offer coach excursions to Keukenhof and the bulbfields, and these can be booked at the VVV Tourist Information Office in Amsterdam. Or buy a day-trip ticket (Rail Idee) from Amsterdam Centraal Station; includes bus transfers from Haarlem and admission charges.
Tourist information: Grachtweg 53A, Lisse. Tel: (0252) 414 262.
Keukenhof tel: (0252) 465 555; www.keukenhof.nl Open: late Mar–May, daily 8am–7.30pm (last admission 6pm).
Museum de Zwarte Tulp tel: (0252) 417 900; www.museumdezwartetulp.nl Open: Tue–Sun 1–5pm.

The bulb-growing heart of The Netherlands

Leiden

Leiden is a likeable university town whose numerous museums will fill a full day. The university, the oldest in The Netherlands, was founded in 1574 by William the Silent as a reward for the town's stoicism in the face of a year-long siege by the Spanish. The siege ended only when William broke the dykes around the town, enabling his ships to sail up to the walls on the resulting floodwaters. When the Spanish retreated, the starving citizens climbed the ramparts to find an abandoned iron pot full of spicy beef and vegetable stew; this same dish, *hutspot*, has become the town's culinary speciality.

The university became a major centre of learning and the town still has a studious atmosphere, though its several museums are far from stuffy.

The **Stedelijk Museum de Lakenhal** (Oude Singel 28–32) is a short walk from the station and covers the history of Leiden and especially its cloth-weaving industry, the staple of the local economy until the 18th century. The museum's best-known painting is Lucas van Leyden's *Last Judgement* triptych, and there are numerous rooms furnished in period style, including a kitchen and brewery.

Nearly opposite (on Tweede Binnenvestgracht 1) is the **Molenmuseum de Valk**, an eight-storey windmill built in 1743, and still in working order. This absorbing museum covers the history of windmills in The Netherlands and provides panoramic views of the city.

A third museum, the **Rijksmuseum voor Volkenkunde** (National Ethnology Museum) is a short stroll away (Steenstraat 1). Recently, the museum has been restored thoroughly. The rich collection of the objects (many of them deriving from Dutch colonial trade) is displayed in such a way that the visitor will notice both the similarities and the contrast between cultures.

Just south of the museum, on Morspoort, is another windmill, this

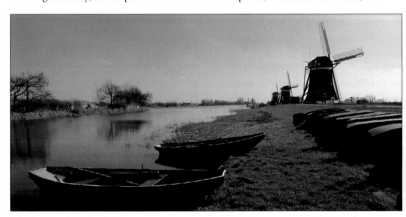

Still life with windmill at Leiden

time a replica of the mill owned by Rembrandt's father, Gerritszoon van Rijn. Rembrandtbrug crosses the River Rijn (Rhine) leading to Weedensteeg where Rembrandt was born in 1606.

By walking down Rembrandtstraat, left into picturesque Groenhazengracht, then right on Rapenburg, you will come to the university district with its handsome classical buildings, notably the Bibliotheca Thysiana of 1655.

Further down is the entrance to **Hortus Botanicus** (the Botanical Garden, Rapenburg 73) founded in 1575. This delightful spot includes a reconstruction of the original garden, the Clusiustuin, named after the garden's former director, Carolus Clusius, the botanist who first introduced bulbs to The Netherlands.

Another famous Leiden citizen is buried in **Pieterskerk**, on the opposite side of Rapenburg. He is John Robinson, a Puritan refugee from England who settled in Leiden in 1609. He became the leader of the Pilgrim Fathers who set sail from Rotterdam in 1620, bound for a new life in the New World. Robinson himself was too ill to join that pioneering voyage and died not long after.

St Pieterskerk is surrounded by the narrow lanes of the medieval quarter, and lined by bookshops and peaceful cafés. To the east, Pieterskerkchoorsteeg leads to the main street, Breestraat, and the Renaissance Stadhuis of 1595. To the north, Pieterskerkhof leads to the attractive jumble of buildings that make up Gravensteen, once the court and prison, now the Law Faculty.

Back on Rapenburg you will find the popular Rijksmuseum van Oudheden

(The National Archaeological Museum). An ancient Egyptian temple has been reconstructed at the entrance to the museum, given to the Dutch nation by the Egyptian government. The Temple of Taffeh was originally built in the 1st century AD for the worship of the sun, and converted to Christian use in the 4th century. The museum has a big collection of Egyptian and Roman material and, less glamorous but of greater local relevance, a floor devoted to the archaeology of The Netherlands.
42km southwest of Amsterdam.
Getting there: train to Dan Haaz/
Rotterdam. Journey time 35 minutes.
Tourist information: Stationsweg 2d.
Tel: (0900) 222 2333.

Hortus Botanicus
Rapenburg 73. Tel: (071) 527 7249;
www.hortusleiden.nl. Open: Easter–end Oct,
daily 10am–6pm; end-Oct–Easter, Sun–Fri
10am–4pm. Closed: Sat, 3 Oct & 25 Dec.
Admission charge.
Molenmuseum de Valk
Binnenvestgracht 1. Tel: (071) 516 5353.
Open: Tue–Sat 10am–5pm, Sun 1–5pm.
Closed: Mon, 1 Jan, 3 Oct & 25 Dec.
Admission charge.
Pieterskerk
Kloksteeg. Open: daily 1.30–4pm.
Free admission.
Rijksmuseum van Oudheden
Rapenburg 28. Tel: (071) 516 3163;
www.rmo.nl. Open: Tue–Fri 10am–5pm,
Sat, Sun & public holidays noon–5pm.
Admission charge.
Rijksmuseum voor Volkenkunde
Steenstraat 1. Tel: (071) 516 8800;
www.rmv.nl. Open: Tue–Sun 10am–5pm.
Admission charge.
Stedelijk Museum de Lakenhal
Oude Singel 28–32. Tel: (071) 516 5360;
www.lakenhal.nl. Open: Tue–Fri 10am–5pm,
Sat–Sun noon–5pm.

Marken

Of all the villages on the IJsselmeer north of Amsterdam, Marken is the quietest and most appealing. The local people have reluctantly turned to tourism to save their economy but they remain proud of their distinctive local traditions. Until 1957, Marken was an island, accessible only by boat, and the population of 200 formed an enclosed, strictly Calvinist community largely untouched by the modern world. The way of life of this fishing village began to change with the building of a causeway in 1957 which provided a link to the mainland. Today the population has been increased by incomers to around 2,000.

Long isolation led to a distinctive style of architecture. The pristine wooden houses lining the harbour are a favourite subject for photographers; they are built on stilts as a flood precaution and linked by timber boardwalks. The clapboard façades are painted green and white, while bright red awnings, and scarlet geraniums add to the colourful effect – even the boats moored in the harbour are painted in the same bright colours. Local people still wear traditional costume, especially on religious feast days, and a distinctive feature is the *ryglyf*, a bodice embroidered with intricate floral motifs. Marken has all the appearance of an open-air museum, but it is a living village of real

Marken is marked by a distinctive style of archictecture and culture

atmosphere. Many visitors fall in love with its quiet charms, especially by contrast with the more commercialised village of Volendam, which can be reached from Marken by means of a half-hour boat trip.

18km northeast of Amsterdam.
Getting there: bus 111 from Amsterdam Centraal Station, or by boat, the Marken Express, from Volendam or Monnickendam. Tourist information: in Edam, Damplein 1. Tel: (0299) 315 125; www.vvv-edam.nl

Monnickendam

Monnickendam has been described as Amsterdam in miniature. Though little more than a village today it has some remarkable buildings surviving from a time when Monnickendam was an important trading centre.

The triple-naved **Grote Kerk** dates from the 15th century, and has a fine oak choir screen of 1563. In the narrow lanes of the harbour area, the 15th-century **Speeltoren**, or Clock Tower, now serves as the local museum (**Museum de Speeltoren**, Noordeine 4); the original clockwork knights in white armour still parade on the hour when the clock carillon plays its delightful tune.

Streets such as Burgwallen, Kerkstraat and Noordeinde are lined by attractive 17th-century houses.

Like other towns on the IJsselmeer, Monnickendam lost its outlet to the sea when the Zuider Zee was dammed, but the enterprising local people quickly turned their hands to fish processing, specialising in smoked herrings and plump eels. The fragrant smell of woodsmoke lingers in the harbour area

The charming town of Monnickendam

where several old-fashioned and informal cafés serve the local speciality – *Monnickendammer twaalf uurtje*, a platter of delicately smoked fish. Another of the town's attractions is the Marken Express, a boat service linking the town with the nearby villages of Marken and Volendam; boats depart at 45-minute intervals during daylight hours from March to October.

16km north of Amsterdam.
Getting there: bus 111 from Amsterdam Centraal Station. Journey time 30 minutes. Tourist information: Nieuwpoortslaan 15. Tel: (0299) 651 998. Open: Mon–Fri 9am–5pm, Sat 9am–4pm.
Museum de Speeltoren open: Jun–mid-Sept, Mon–Sat 10am–4pm, Sun 1–4pm (mid-Apr–May, Sat–Sun only).

Muiderslot

Muiderslot, also known as Muiden Castle, is a beautiful red-brick building that rises from its moat like the archetypal fairy-tale castle. It was originally built in 1285 by a count of Holland, Floris V, who set the economy of medieval Amsterdam on a sound footing by granting its citizens a 'toll privilege' in 1275; this enabled Amsterdammers to transport their goods along the canals of Holland county without paying tolls. Despite – or because of – this, Floris V was kidnapped, imprisoned and finally murdered in his own castle by a group of noblemen angered by his generosity, which had the effect of undermining their income.

The Bishop of Utrecht, who may have been behind the murder conspiracy, annexed the count's territory and demolished the castle in 1296.

The castle was then rebuilt on the same foundations in 1386, and 300 years later it became the residence of Pieter Hooft. Between 1609 and 1647, Hooft, an illustrious poet and historian, used the castle as a place of philosophical and artistic debate. Here he would entertain the leading poets, artists and intellectuals of his day who became known as the Muiden Circle.

After a period of neglect the castle was thoroughly restored in 1948 and it is now furnished in the style of the early 17th century, as it might have been when Monnickendam was a busy merchant port in the time of Pieter Hooft. The charms of the castle are enhanced by delightful gardens.

12km east of Amsterdam.
Getting there: bus 136 from Amsterdam Amstel station. Journey time 40 minutes. Tel: (0294) 261 325. Open: April–Oct, Mon–Fri 10am–4pm, Sat, Sun & public holidays 1–4pm; Nov–Mar, Sat–Sun 1–4pm. Closed: Mon–Fri. Guided tours only.

Naarden

Naarden suffered a devastating blow in 1572 when the town was sacked by Spanish troops under Don Frederick of Toledo (son of the Duke of Alva) and almost all the inhabitants were massacred. The brutality of the attack only increased Dutch determination to drive the hated Spaniards from their soil. Naarden was left a ghost town until repopulated in the 17th century when, in order to prevent the possibility of another massacre, the town was equipped with state-of-the-art defences, designed by Adriaan Dortsman. As a result, Naarden has some of the best-preserved Renaissance fortifications in Europe and the town resembles an island surrounded by an impressive double moat and bastions. Their story is told in the **Nederlands Vestingmuseum** (Fortification Museum) located in the Turfpoortbastion (Westwalstraat 6). This is no dry museum of military history but an excellent account of 17th-century warfare; there are subterranean passages to explore, and the admission price includes a boat trip around the moats.

The 1572 massacre is commemorated by a plaque on the **Spaanse Huis** (Spanish House, Turfpoortstraat 27), built in 1615. This now houses the

Comeniusmuseum, devoted to the life and theories of the philosopher, Johann Komenski (Comenius), a Moravian refugee who settled in the town in 1621 and laid the foundations of modern educational practice; he abhorred learning by rote and was a pioneering advocate of visual aids.

The **Grote Kerk**, in the centre of the town, fortunately survived the Spanish onslaught. It has a wooden choir screen of 1513 and an unusual set of vault paintings illustrating stories from the Old and New Testaments; the 20 wooden panels, painted between 1510 and 1518, are based on the woodcuts of Dürer. The tower is well worth climbing for a bird's-eye view of the fortifications and of the surrounding Gooiland landscape, an extensive area of woodland, heath and lakes.

21km east of Amsterdam. Getting there: bus 136 from Amsterdam Amstel station. Journey time 55 minutes. Tourist information: Adriaan Dortsmanplein 1B. Tel: (035) 694 2836. Nederlands Vestingmuseum tel: (035) 694 5459. Open: Easter–Oct, Tue–Fri 10.30am–5pm (and Mons in summer), Sat, Sun & public holidays noon–5pm; Nov–Feb, Sun noon–5pm. Grote Kerk open: Jun–Sept daily 1–4pm. Comeniusmuseum tel: (035) 694 3045; www.comeniusmuseum.nl Open: Wed–Sun noon–5pm. Closed: 25 Dec, 31 Dec & 1 Jan.

The turrets and battlements of Muiderslot Castle seem straight from a fairy tale

Rotterdam

Rotterdam was virtually
flattened at the beginning
of World War II when the
Nazis bombed The
Netherlands into
surrender. A new city has
arisen on the old, noted for
its imaginative modern
architecture, excellent
museums and the world's
largest container port.

The rather soulless
centre is the least attractive
part of the city. From the
station cross to the
windswept pedestrian
shopping centre either side
of Coolsingel; putting this
behind, it is best to head
for the waterfront around
Oude Haven where the
most striking of the city's
buildings are located.

The pyramidal
Gemeentebibliotheek
(Central Library) clearly
owes a debt to the
Pompidou Centre in Paris
with its external ducting
and polished steel. Take a
ride on the escalators for
views over the old port and
of the internal hanging
gardens. Alongside are the
unusual cube houses
designed by Piet Blom; one
of them, the **Kijk-Kubus**
(Overblaak 70) is open to
the public and well worth a
visit even if you conclude
that the giddying wall

angles and the specially
adapted furniture make
these futuristic houses
rather a strain to live in.
The complex includes a
shop-lined bridge based on
the Ponte Vecchio in
Florence and the wharf is
lined with pleasant cafés.

Further along the boat-
filled harbour is the
**Maritiem Museum
Rotterdam**, devoted to the
city's maritime history. The
museum ship *De Buffel*,
moored alongside, is a
19th-century warship with
surprisingly luxurious
officers' quarters. If you
continue down Leuvehaven
you will come to the
harbourside offices of
Spido Havenrondvaarten,
the departure point for
boat tours of the
Europoort. Further along
the waterfront is a
distinguished classical

THE EUROPOORT

Rotterdam's Europoort
stretches for 37km
along the Nieuwe Maas
river and handles some
4 per cent of the world's
container traffic. Cargo
unloaded here is
transported deep into the
heart of Europe along
three great rivers, the
Rhine, the Maas (Meuse)
and the Scheldt. Every
year around 32,000 ships
dock and unload their
containers – laid end to
end they would stretch
for 563,200km. These
and other overwhelming
statistics come to life if
you take one of the 75-
minute Spido harbour
tours which depart from
Leuvehoofd regularly
during the day.
Tel: (010) 275 9988.

The new bridge at Rotterdam

Maritiem Museum of Rotterdam

building, formerly the Royal Dutch Yacht Club, now a museum of ethnography, the **Wereldmuseum**.

Towering above the adjacent park is the **Euromast**, begun in 1958 for the Floriade flower festival and originally 104m high. The Space Tower was added in 1970 bringing the total height to 185m. External lifts climb to the revolving Space Cabin at the summit where the views take in the whole 37-km waterfront of the Europoort.

Totally different in scale is the Delfshaven district alongside, which escaped bombing and is lined with 18th- and 19th-century warehouses converted to chic apartments.

The Pilgrim Fathers sailed from here in 1620 in the *Speedwell*; this ship proved unseaworthy and so, after docking at Plymouth, the religious refugees continued to the New World in the *Mayflower*.

The **Historische Museum Rotterdam de Dubbelde Palmboom** (Voorhaven 12) explains the history of the area and its industries.

Returning to the city centre, the **Museum Boijmans Van Beuningen** (Museumpark 18–20) contains one of Europe's most important art collections. Three sections of this vast museum are a must: the rooms dedicated to early Dutch painting contain Pieter Bruegel's *Tower of Babel* and several works by Hieronymus Bosch; rooms 36 and 37 are devoted to the work of Rembrandt and his pupils; rooms 25 to 30 contain a collection of Surrealistic paintings, including works by Dali, Magritte and Ernst.

76km southwest of Amsterdam.
Getting there: train to Rotterdam Coolsingel 67. Journey time 60 minutes.
Tourist information: Coolsingel 67.
Tel: (0900) 403 4065;
www.vvv.rotterdam.nl

Historische Museum Rotterdam de Dubbelde Palmboom
Voorhaven 12. Tel: (010) 217 6767; www.hmr.rotterdam.nl. Open: Tue–Fri 10am–5pm, Sat, Sun & public holidays 11am–5pm. Admission charge.

Euromast
Parkhaven 20. Tel: (010) 436 4811; www.euromast.nl. Open: daily, Oct–Mar 10am–11pm, Apr–Sept 9.30am–11pm. Admission charge.

Kijk-Kubus
Overblaak 70. Tel: (010) 414 2285; www.cubehouse.nl. Open: Jan–Feb Fri–Sun 11am–5pm, Mar–Dec daily 11am–5pm. Admission charge.

Maritiem Museum Rotterdam
Leuvehaven 1. Tel: (010) 413 2680; www.maritiemmuseum.nl. Open: Tue–Sat 10am–5pm, Sun & public holidays 11am–5pm; also Mon 10am–5pm in Jul & Aug. Admission charge.

Museum Boijmans Van Beuningen
Museumpark 18–20. Tel: (010) 441 9400; www.boijmans.rotterdam.nl. Open: Tue–Sat 10am–5pm, Sun & public holidays 11am–5pm. Admission charge.

Wereldmuseum Rotterdam
Willemskade 25. Tel: (010) 270 7172; www.wereldmuseum.rotterdam.nl. Open: Tue–Sun 10am–5pm. Closed 1 Jan, 30 Apr, 25 Dec. Admission charge.

Utrecht

Utrecht is one of the oldest cities in The Netherlands, founded in AD 47 as a Roman garrison town to protect a strategic ford across the River Rhine. Pepin the Short, father of Charlemagne, made Utrecht a bishopric in the 7th century and the city became the main religious centre of the northern Dutch provinces in the Middle Ages, its skyline bristling with the spires of numerous churches and convents. Many were destroyed by a hurricane that hit the town in 1674. Those that remain range in style from Romanesque to High Gothic, several of them now converted to museums.

On arriving in Utrecht visitors first have to negotiate the intrusive 1970s' Hoog Catharijne office and shopping complex which stands between the station and the old city. Head for **Oude Gracht**, an unusual sunken canal built in two tiers to accommodate the tidal extremes of the Rhine. The lower quay is lined with cavernous cellars, many now turned into cafés and restaurants. Some of Utrecht's oldest buildings line the canal; the Huis Oudaen (No. 99) dates from 1320 and Drakenborch (No. 114) was built in 1280.

Follow the canal south heading for the unmissable landmark of the **Domtoren** (Cathedral Tower), a lacy Gothic masterpiece completed in 1382 and soaring to 112m. Some contemporaries dismissed the tower as a symbol of vanity and pride, predicting that it would surely collapse. In fact, it was the cathedral which came crashing to the ground in the 1674 hurricane, leaving only the choir of 1321, modelled on Cologne Cathedral, and the 15th-century cloister.

The cathedral was conceived as the centrepiece of an ambitious scheme

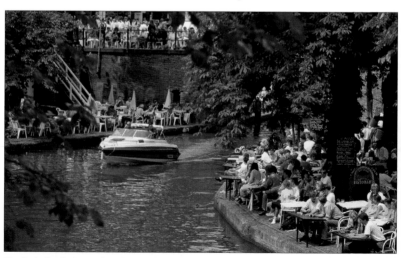

The Oude Gracht in Utrecht is lined with old buildings and restaurants

devised by Bishop Bernold in the mid-11th century. He drew up a plan to build five churches, one at each of the four cardinal points of the compass and the cathedral in the centre, together forming the shape of the cross. Only two of the five were completed in Bernold's lifetime: to the east of the Domkerk is **Pieterskerk**, built in Romanesque style in 1048, while to the north is **Janskerk**, completed in 1050, and given a new Gothic choir in the 16th century.

From Janskerk, follow the canal delightfully called Drift and then turn left down Kromme Nieuwegracht; this canal follows the original course of the Rhine and is lined with elegant 18th-century houses. It leads to picturesque Pausdam and the late-Gothic **Paushuisje** (Pope's House), built in 1517 for Adriaan Floriszoon. He never saw the house, having spent most of his time in Spain as tutor to Charles V and then as the Bishop of Tortosa. In 1622 he became Adrian VI, the first and only Dutch pope – a short-lived reign, as he died the following year.

Nieuwegracht leads south to a former Carmelite convent, now the **Museum Catharijneconvent Utrecht**, whose excellent medieval paintings and sculptures are part of a collection illustrating the history of religion in The Netherlands. Further south, the **Centraal Museum**, housed in another medieval convent, has an eclectic range of exhibits, ranging from period rooms, costumes and doll's houses, to the Renaissance paintings of the Utrecht artist Jan van Scorel, and the colourful modern furniture of the de Stijl

movement architect Gerrit Rietveld. Train enthusiasts should not miss the **Nederlands Spoorwegmuseum** (Railway Museum), housed nearby in the disued 19th-century station.

The best route back to the city centre is through the park alongside Stads-buitengracht, formerly the moat of the medieval city walls, then up Springweg to Buurkerkhof. This 13th-century church now houses the **Nationaal Museum Van Speelklok tot Pierement** (meaning From Musical Clocks to Street Organs), an enchanting museum of mechanical musical instruments.
35km south of Amsterdam.
Getting there: train to Utrech CS.
Journey time 30 minutes.
Tourist information: Vinkenburgstraat 19.
Tel: (0900) 128 8732;
www.utrechtstad.com

Centraal Museum
Agnietenstraat 1. Tel: (030) 236 2362;
www.centraalmuseum.nl. Open: Tue–Sun
11am–5pm. Admission charge.
Domtoren
Domplein. Tel: (030) 286 4540.
Open: Mon–Sat 10am–4pm, Sun noon–4pm.
Admission charge.
Nationaal Museum Van Speelklok tot Pierement
Buurkerkhof 10. Tel: (030) 231 2789;
www.museumspeelklok.nl. Open: Tue–Sat
10am–5pm, Sun & public holidays
noon–5pm. Admission charge.
Nederlands Spoorwegmuseum
Maliebaanstation. Tel: (030) 230 6206;
www.spoorwegmuseum.nl. Open: Tue–Sun
10am–5pm, also Mon during school
holidays. Closed 1 Jan. Admission charge.
Museum Catharijneconvent Utrecht
Nieuwegracht 63. Tel: (030) 231 7296;
www.catharijneconvent.nl. Open: Tue–Fri
10am–5pm, Sat, Sun & public holidays
11am–5pm. Admission charge.

Volendam

The former fishing village of Volendam is now a highly commercialised tourist attraction, to be avoided by those who do not like crowds and shops full of kitsch souvenirs (go to quieter Marken or Monnickendam instead). On the other hand, it is fun for children and the local people are friendly, wholehearted participants in this recreation of 'old world' Holland. Like actors in a living theme park, they pose for photographers in village costume – baggy black trousers for the men and winged lace caps, flowered dresses and striped aprons for the women. Visitors are also welcome to dress up in costume and have their pictures taken. The harbour is lined with picturesque wooden houses, no two alike, and the **Volendams Museum** (Kloostervuurt 5) tells the story of the ups and downs of the local fishing industry.

18km northeast of Amsterdam.
Getting there: bus 110, 112 & 116 from Amsterdam Centraal Station. Journey time 30 minutes. Or buy a day-trip excursion ticket *which includes the bus journey to Edam, plus boat transfers to Marken and Volendam.*
Tourist information: Zeestraat 37. Tel: (0299) 363 747; www.vvv-volendam.nl; Volendams Museum open: daily, Apr–Oct 10am–5pm.

Zaanse Schans

The former villages of Zaandam, Koog aan de Zaan and Zaandijk, north of Amsterdam, all take their names from the River Zaan on whose banks they sit. An industrial revolution of a kind occurred here in the 16th century with the invention of a wind-powered sawmill: the area became the biggest supplier of timber for shipbuilding and house construction in The Netherlands. When Monet came here to paint the scene in the 1870s there were over 1,000 windmills producing everything from corn and mustard to paint pigments and vegetable oil. Development has continued and the former villages have merged to form the Zaanstad conurbation. In the 1950s, many of the

The national footwear as worn in Zaanse Schans

surviving windmills were moved to the Zaanse Schans, located on the river bank opposite Zaandijk. An unusual feature of the open-air museum is that people actually live in its houses and windmills, and several of the mills continue to produce mustard and flour. They are maintained in pristine working order by enthusiasts who are dedicated to keeping traditional milling skills alive and who lovingly demonstrate the complex workings of these elegant machines. The museum also has several streets of 17th-century timber-gabled houses where visitors can watch craft demonstrations, and take a boat trip along the River Zaan.

14km north of Amsterdam.
Getting there: train from Amsterdam
Centraal Station to Koog-Zaandijk.
Journey time 15 minutes.
Tourist information: Gedempte Gracht
76, Zaandam. Tel: (075) 616 2221.
Zaanse Schaus tel: (075) 616 8218;
www.zaanseschans.nl
Open: daily 9am–5pm.

Zandvoort

On hot summer days when Amsterdammers feel like a cooling dip in the sea they head for Zandvoort, a popular coastal resort but big enough to accommodate the crowds with ease. The busiest beaches are those closest to Zandvoort town, whose northern quarter has been conserved and retains the atmosphere of a fishing village. The modern part of the town has numerous fish restaurants, and a casino (Badhuisplaats) worth a visit just for the views. Sandy and gently shelving beaches stretch for miles either side of

Zandvoort: a nearby getaway for Amsterdammers

the town and you will find privacy if you walk far enough. Nature lovers should head south to the **Waterleidingduinen**, an undulating dune reserve where horned poppy and sea holly grow in the sheltered lee of the shifting sandbanks.

25km west of Amsterdam.
Getting there: train from Amsterdam
Centraalstation to Zandvoort aan Zee.
Journey time 24 minutes. Tourist
information: Schoolplein 1.
Tel: (023) 571 7947; www.vvvzk.nl

Vanished lives are recreated at the Zuiderzee
Museum

Enkhuizen

The fascinating story of the reclamation
of the Zuiderzee and of the vanished
way of life of its former fishing villages
is told at the **Zuiderzeemuseum** in
Enkhuizen. Drainage of the Zuider Zee
began as early as the 17th century with
the creation of the Beemster, Purmer
and Wormer polders. Dykes were built
to hold back the sea, and drainage canals
were dug; windmills, fitted with scoop
wheels, were then used to raise the water
high enough to flow back into the sea.
The land thus reclaimed was very fertile;
villages surrounding the Zuiderzee
became wealthy on the profits from
arable crops, adding to their income
from marine trade and fishing, and they
built imposing town halls to celebrate
their new prosperity.

By the mid-18th century, the sea had
silted up to the extent that big ships
could no longer reach Amsterdam,
a problem resolved by digging the
Noordzee Kanaal, which opened in
1876. The widespread use of steam
pumps from the mid-19th century
added impetus to land reclamation, but
the new fields were always liable to
flooding from the combined forces of
high tides and heavy rainfall. After a
devastating flood that occurred in 1916,
a long-standing plan to dam the
Zuiderzee, first mooted by the engineer
Cornelis Lely in 1891, was revived. The
Afsluitdijk (Enclosing Dyke) was built
by sinking woven willow mattresses to
act as a raft, thus preventing the huge
weight of stones and concrete piled on
top from sinking into the sea bed. When
the dyke was completed in 1932, flags
flew at half mast in the port towns
round the shore, which were now cut off
from the sea.

The old tidal Zuiderzee became a
shallow inland lake and was rechristened
the IJsselmeer. By subdividing the lake
with further dams, huge areas of
marshland were drained and seeded
with grass to draw off the salt before
being turned over to agriculture. In this
way the new province of Flevoland was
created and its capital, named Lelystad
after the 19th-century engineer, received
its first settlers in 1967.

Enkhuizen was one of the ports to
suffer from an abrupt end to its former
way of life; it had once been the
foremost herring port in The
Netherlands. As compensation for the
loss of income, it was chosen as the site
for the splendid Zuiderzeemuseum

(Wierdijk) – two museums, in fact, consisting of the indoor **Binnenmuseum**, opened in 1950, and the open-air Buitenmuseum, opened in 1983.

The Binnenmuseum is located in a splendid Renaissance building built on the waterfront in 1625 and known as the Peperhuis because, under Dutch East India Company ownership, it had been used for storing pepper imported from Indonesia. Room 1 of the museum houses a collection of historic Zuiderzee fishing boats, rooms 4 to 7 are devoted to locally made furniture and rooms 13 to 15 to traditional costume. It is clear from the exhibits that each village developed its own distinctive style, not just in dress but even in shipbuilding techniques, a reflection of the fact that these villages, though only a few miles apart, were rivals for trade and emphasised their differences in numerous ways.

The open-air museum is, appropriately enough, reached by boat which passes among the traditional sailing craft moored in the harbour. The museum consists of more than 130 buildings reconstructed to form complete streets modelled on the towns from which they were rescued; thus you can walk from Monnickendam to Edam, from Edam to Amsterdam, and from the city to the more rural village of Staveren in the course of a few hours. Informative labelling explains the history of each building and its former occupants. Many are furnished in period style or used to demonstrate crafts, such as baking, herring curing, tanning and rope making.

If the museums do not keep you occupied for a whole day, you can always take a boat trip from the harbour (summer only) to **Medemblik**, with its steam train museum, which offers a steam train service to Hoorn, and 13th-century castle, or to **Urk**, with its Visserijmuseum (Fishing Museum) and excellent fish restaurants.

64km northeast of Amsterdam.
Getting there: train from Amsterdam Centraal Station to Enkhuizen. Journey time 60 minutes.
Tourist information: Tussen Twee Havens. Tel: (0228) 313 164; www.vvweb.nl
Zuiderzeemuseum tel: (0228) 351 111; www.zuiderzeemuseum.nl
Indoor museum open: daily 10am–5pm.
Outdoor museum open: Apr–Oct, Tue–Sun 10am–5pm (also Mon in Jul & Aug).

Mackerel hung for smoking

Getting Away From It All

The unspoilt beauty of
Amsterdamse Bos

*'I like to wander through the old narrow and rather
sombre streets with their shops occupied by chemists,
lithographers and ship's chandlers and browse among
the navigation charts and other ship's supplies.
I cannot tell you how beautiful the area is at twilight.'*
VINCENT VAN GOGH

Amsterdamse Bos
(Amsterdam Wood)

Amsterdam Wood, on the southern
fringes of the city, is the product of the
Great Depression of the 1930s. To
resolve the problem of mass
unemployment, the city decided to
convert 895 hectares of polder into a
recreation park modelled on the Bois de
Boulogne in Paris. No machinery was
used in making the park, so as to create
the maximum number of jobs.

The park is man-made in a very real
sense: teams of men and horses laid
310km of drainage pipe to lower the
water table by 1.5m so that the
thousands of trees they planted would
develop strong roots. They dug the
Roeibaan, a 2-km rowing lake, created
an artificial hill to act as a viewpoint and
laid over 200km of footpaths and cycle
tracks.

The result today is a mature park,
beautifully maintained, where visitors
can escape the crowds and wander along
tree-shaded paths, picnic in sunny
glades or by the lakeside, hire a bicycle,
go canoeing or swim in the lake. Those
who simply want to walk can follow the
Roeibaan to its furthest point and visit
the Bosmuseum (Woodland Museum)

which explains how the park was
built and illustrates all its flora and
fauna, from squirrels and songbirds
to fungi and 700 different beetle
species.
Entrance: Bosmuseum, Koenenkade 56.
Tel: (020) 676 2152.
Park open: 24 hours.
Museum open: daily 10am–5pm.
Free admission.
Bus: 170, 171 & 172. Or take tram 6 or
16, or bus 15, to Haarlemmermeer
station and ride to the park on an
old-fashioned tram.
(Services every Sun, Apr–Oct, also
Tue–Sat in Jul–Aug; see Electrische
Museumtramlijn, pp47–8 for details.)

Hortus Botanicus Plantage
(Botanical Garden)

Laid out in 1682 as a medicinal garden,
it soon evolved into a showcase for the
many new plants that Dutch explorers
brought back from the Far East. In 1706,
it became the first place outside Arabia
to cultivate the coffee plant.

The main features of this garden are a
Palm House of iron and glass with aerial
walkways, which houses the world's
oldest pot plant, a 400-year-old palm, an
Orangery where you can enjoy coffee

and cakes, a herb garden in the 17th-century style, a huge hothouse which incorporates three different tropical climates, a special area for carnivorous plants, a rock garden, a Japanese garden and an educational house.

Plantage Middenlaan 2.
Tel: (020) 625 9021; www.dehortus.nl
Mon–Fri opens 9am, Sat–Sun opens
10am, closes daily at 4pm in Dec–Jan,
9pm in Jul–Aug, and 5pm other months.
Closed: 1 Jan & 25 Dec.
Admission charge.
Trams: 7, 9 & 14. Nearby: Zoo (Artis).

Hortus Botanicus Van de Vrije Universiteit (Botanical Garden of the Free University)

This garden was planted in 1967. It has an interesting section devoted to the native flora of The Netherlands, large areas of woodland and glasshouses devoted to cold, temperate or tropical-climate plants.

Van der Boechorststraat 8. Tel: (020) 444
9390; www.vv.nl/hortus Open: Mon–Fri
8am–4.30pm also Jul–Aug Sat 9am–5pm.
Free admission. Buses: 23, 65, 170, 171,
172 & 199. Nearby: Amsterdamse Bos.

An ambitious development programme will make the Botanical Garden even more of a must for green-minded visitors

Cost effective, 'green' family transport

Cycle Routes

Every year thousands of visitors to Amsterdam are seduced into believing that 'cycling is the ideal means of transport in Amsterdam'. They hire a bike and then wish they had not. Cycling in Amsterdam is a hair-raising experience; bike-riding natives are a law unto themselves: everybody seems to ignore the traffic rules, including pedestrians, and when you reach for your brakes you often find they are not there – many Dutch bikes are the old-fashioned kind which you have to back pedal to stop. Bicycles are also a favourite target of thieves who find ways of removing even the most securely locked bikes. With practice all these problems can be overcome, but if you do choose to cycle in Amsterdam, dismount at busy intersections and cross on foot, and secure your bike to an immovable object if you leave it in the street.

By contrast, cycling in the Dutch countryside is a joy, especially in summer when there is no wind to fight against. The rider has the choice of over 10,000km of specially designated cycle paths (*fietspaden*), which are clearly marked on ANWB 1:100,000 scale maps and well signposted on the ground. Road and cycleway intersections are usually numbered so you can always find out where you are on the map. VVV Tourist Information Centres also supply informative maps of local cycle routes. You can hire bicycles at almost any railway station – a system designed to discourage people from taking their own bikes on the trains. Simply present your ticket if you have one and some means of identification, such as a passport, at the ticket office; you will be charged a small refundable deposit and a negligible hire fee; children's bikes and bikes with child seats can also be hired.

Several nature reserves within easy reach of Amsterdam offer traffic-free cycling conditions, as well as scenic landscapes, picnic spots and wildlife. From the station at Castricum (26km northwest of Amsterdam; journey time 30 minutes) you are within easy reach of the **North Holland Dunes**, an extensive area of sand and shingle bank backed by thick woodland. Johanna's Hof, at the highest point in the woods, is a very popular destination because of its pancakes and small zoo.

To the east of Amsterdam you can take a train to **Hilversum** (20km; journey time 20 minutes) and explore the extensive heath and woodland of the Bussummerheide and Boswachterij De Lage Vuumsche, heading for the pancake houses in the village of Lage Vuursche when you are hungry.

The rolling hills and moors of the **Nationaal Park Hoge Veluwe**, north of Arnhem (*see p102*) are ideal for cycling and free bikes, painted white, are available for anyone to use within the confines of the vast park. Hoge Veluwe has the added attraction of its open-air **Sculpture Garden** and the **Kröller-Müller Museum**, featuring over 200 Van Gogh paintings.

Once confident enough to cope with the roads, you could visit the IJsselmeer villages of Marken and Monnickendam (*see pp118–9*) by bike instead of by bus or coach (maps available from the Amsterdam VVV). If you hire a bike at Amsterdam Centraal Station, you can cross the IJ harbour by free passenger ferry. The ferry departs regularly from the harbour side of the station (signposted Pont naar Tolhuis). You will initially encounter traffic on the northern bank but, as you cycle east along Durgerdammerdijk, the suburbs give way to open countryside dotted with red-roofed farmhouses and you may spot herons wading in the watercourses.

The route passes through Durgerdam, an attractive former fishing village, then along the shores of the IJsselmeer to Uitdam; 3km further on is the causeway to the island village of **Marken** with its painted wooden houses, and beyond lies **Monnickendam**, 'Amsterdam in miniature'.

The return journey is through **Broek in Waterland**, a town of spotless beauty and a major centre of cheese production, where the informal restaurant, De Witte Swaen, is used by hungry cyclists. From here the road through Zunderdorp will bring you back to the IJ ferry. Allow at least four hours for the 34-km round trip.

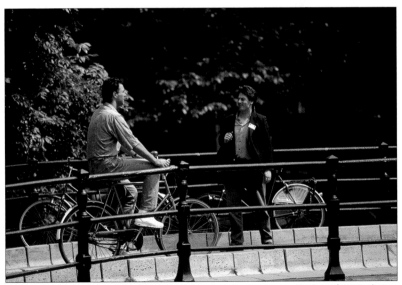

The humble bicycle has found its niche in the flat, narrow streets, alleys and bridges of Amsterdam

Maritime exhibits in the Rykers Museum at Den Helder

Den Helder and the Waddenzee

From Amsterdam Centraal Station it is only an hour by train to Den Helder, a port town on the edge of a truly wild corner of The Netherlands renowned for its bird and marine life. Ferries from Den Helder cross to the island of Texel, the first and largest of the five Frisian (or Wadden) Islands which extend in a broad curve eastwards to the German coast. These islands, and the submerged sandbars in between, act as a natural breakwater, separating the shallow waters of the Waddenzee to the east from the rough and often stormy North Sea to the west.

The Waddenzee covers an area of almost 2,600sq km, but is nowhere more than 3m deep, even at high tide. As the tide goes out the sea rolls away to expose an extensive area of mudflats rich in marine molluscs, worms and the spawn of numerous North Sea fish. This in turn attracts huge feeding flocks of gulls, waders and wildfowl.

Den Helder itself was a fishing village until Napoleon fortified it as a naval base in 1808, and it remains the headquarters of the Dutch naval fleet. Ferries to Texel depart from the harbour at hourly intervals all through the year and the crossing takes 20 minutes.

From the island port of 't Horntje, buses go to **Den Burg**, the main village, where visitors can hire bicycles, see the local museum and then call at the VVV Tourist Information Centre (*Emmalaan 66, tel: (0222) 314 741*) for a guide to cycle routes and to the island's numerous bird sanctuaries. **De Koog**, on the western side of Texel, is the island's main resort and has a small natural history centre, the Ecomare, with a bird and seal sanctuary and aquarium, but the best spots for birdwatching lie to the south and east, below Den Hoorn.

Depending on the season, visitors should look out for waders such as curlews, oystercatchers, plovers, redshanks, greenshanks and stints, as well as pintail ducks, shelducks, teal, terns and geese. Sadly, the grey seals that were once so common are now a rare sight. A viral disease has decimated the population and the remaining colonies are limited to the less-populated of the Frisian Islands.

Island Hopping and Mudwalking

The best way to explore the **Frisian Islands** is by hiring an antique sailing boat for the week or a weekend, complete with crew and sleeping accommodation (*details from Rederij Vooruit, Geeuwkade 9, 8651 AA IJ1st; tel: (0515) 531 485; www.rederij-vooruit.nl*). Otherwise the islands can be reached only by separate ferries from the mainland.

You can also walk to some of the islands on *wadlopen* (mudwalking) excursions during summer, but for that you must be physically fit, and quite prepared to get very muddy: wading up to your thighs in mud is as demanding as mountain climbing. It is dangerous to cross the mudflats on your own, so join a party led by an officially licensed guide if you want a close encounter with the rich and varied ecology of the Waddenzee (*details from Dijkstra's Wadlooptochten, Hoofdstraat 118, 9968 AM Pieterburen, tel: (0595) 528 345*).

As a rule, the five Frisian Islands become smaller, wilder and more remote from civilisation the further north you travel, although they can be busy on summer weekends when sunbathers and windsurfers pour out of the cities to enjoy them.

Texel is the only island where visitors will encounter cars in any number. **Vlieland** (reached by ferry from Harlingen) is popular with birdwatchers and naturists – it has the biggest nudist beach in Europe.

Terschelling, the middle island (also reached from Harlingen) once guarded the main shipping lanes into the Zuider Zee; numerous ships were wrecked on its shifting sandbanks, including the *Lutine*, whose bell, the only part recovered, is still rung at Lloyd's, the London insurance market, whenever a ship is declared lost at sea.

Mudlarks off on the trail

Shopping

Amsterdam, a city built on commerce, seems at first glance to have surprisingly few shops, until you realise that they are, very sensibly, tucked away on pedestrianised side streets or along the short radial canals that link the three main canals of the Grachtengordel. Here you will find all sorts of surprises: Amsterdam's shopkeepers are masters of the art of window display and there are many small speciality shops that sell a single product in all its varieties.

Amsterdam shops cater for all tastes

It is easy to spend a whole day shopping or browsing and not be bored. Thursday is best, as the shops stay open until 9pm. Saturday is the busiest day, but shops close promptly at 5pm and many do not reopen until 1pm (department stores 11am) on Monday. Increasingly, shops are opening on Sunday, usually from noon to 5pm, but few shops are open on Monday morning. Otherwise, normal shopping hours are between 9am and 6pm, and most major credit cards are universally accepted.

SHOPPING IN THE CENTRE

Damrak, the main street, is dominated by fast-food outlets and souvenir shops, but Allert de Lange, Damrak 62, is an oasis of civilisation, stocking a good range of books in several European languages.

Further up, De Bijenkorf (The Beehive) is the Harrods of Amsterdam, selling everything from Delftware to handmade chocolates, though you may find certain clothes cheaper at the **C & A** and **Peek & Cloppenburg** stores on Damrak and Dam Square, respectively.

Parallel to Damrak is Nieuwendijk, a crowded pedestrian precinct lined with cheap clothes shops and brightly-lit stalls selling doughnuts and nougat that would not look out of place in a fairground.

Just behind Nieuwe Kerk, on Nieuwezijds Voorburgwal 137–9, is a delightful shop which captures the magic of Christmas even in the heat of summer; Christmas World sells nothing but old-fashioned tree decorations, stocking fillers and toys. Opposite, the former main Post Office has been turned into the up-market 200-shop **Magna Plaza** galleria providing a new shopping focus to the city.

Kalverstraat, the main shopping street, runs from Dam Square to Muntplein. Competition between traders is fierce and there are many bargains to be had if you shop around in the high street fashion stores. **The American Book Center**, No. 185, has a huge stock of paperbacks and children's books at genuine bargain prices. Some well-known multinational chains also have branches here: **Hennes & Mauritz** at No. 125, **Body Shop** at Nos 157–9 and **Waterstone's Booksellers** at No. 152. At the junction of Kalverstraat and Spui is the splendid Empire-style building recently given a hi-tech interior for the fashion chain, Esprit.

On Muntplein, alongside the Munttoren, is **De Porceleyne Fles**, the official outlet for genuine handpainted Delftware, marked on the base with the letter D, a considerably superior product to the cheap mass-produced blue and white pottery sold as Delft in many souvenir shops.

A few steps away, on Singel, is the **Bloemenmarkt** (Flower Market), where 15 florists sell bulbs, seeds, floral bouquets and even clipped box topiary from floating stalls. The florists can advise on customs regulations concerning the import of plant materials and will arrange shipping.

Turning left at the end of Singel brings you to Koningsplein and Leidsestraat, another busy shopping thoroughfare. The highlight here is **Metz & Co**, which sells the products of top international designers – furniture, fabrics, kitchenware, glass and smaller gift items such as ornaments and toiletries.

The striking Post-Modernist café on the top floor is an excellent place to rest your weary feet and enjoy the fine views.

The Beehive is a honeypot for shoppers

Albert Cuypstraat is the venue for Amsterdam's main market (Mon–Sat 9.30am–5pm), a crowded, colourful, and vibrant affair attended by up to 50,000 people on a typical Saturday. The stalls and milling crowds stretch for nearly a mile, making this Europe's biggest general market. It occupies the heart of the district known as the 'Pijp' – the Pipe – because the long, narrow and slightly curving streets resemble the stem of an old-fashioned clay pipe.

The market has a festive social air because people come here to be seen and to meet friends as much as to shop. The eye is one moment diverted by the stalls piled high with exotic fish and vegetables, colourful cheeses and bolts of fabric, the next by the passing parade of people of all the races that make up this multi-ethnic city.

Albert Cuypstraat sells useful things – clothes, food, even livestock and pets – whereas Amsterdam's other big market, on Waterlooplein (Mon–Sat 9am–5pm) is a flea market in the very real sense, but it still makes for fascinating browsing and just occasionally you might pick up an Art Deco vase, a mirror or some knick-knack that you cannot resist. Bargaining over the price is all part of the fun. Amsterdam has several other markets along the same lines, selling junk and near antiques – on Noordermarkt every Monday from 7.30am to 1pm, on

Nieuwmarkt (May–Sept, Sun 9am–5pm) and in the indoor arcade called Antiekcentrum de Looier, entered from Elandsgracht 109 (Sat–Thur 11am–5pm). Less well known by visitors, but interesting, are the Sunday art markets

held on the Spui and Thorbeckeplein (both Apr–Nov only, 10am–6pm).

Stamp and coin collectors should visit the specialist market on Nieuwezijds Voorburgwal (Wed & Sat 1–4pm), while the covered arcade of the Oudemanhuispoort is a permanent market for second-hand books, mostly in Dutch (open: Mon–Sat 10am–4pm).

Finally, all self-respecting greens and ecologists do their weekly shopping at the Boerenmarkt (Farmers' Market) on Noordermarkt (Sat 9am–4pm, 3pm in winter) where all the produce on sale is organic.

Ironically there is another, far from ecological, market alongside; the weekly pet market.

Facing page above: many visitors look for traditional clogs to take home; below: local cheese
Above: Jenever bottles
Left: Waterlooplein market is a fascinating place to browse for exotica

A tight spot?

SPECIALITY SHOPS

Characterful small shops are to be found all over Amsterdam, especially along the quiet, village-like streets of the Canal Circle or in chic PC Hooftstraat in the Museum Quarter. Here you are likely to find just the gift (for yourself, or for friends) that proved so elusive in the busier shopping thoroughfares. This directory is by no means exhaustive, but it does cover some of the most distinctive shops in the city.

Antiques

The Spiegelkwartier is renowned for its concentration of antique shops where you can pick up relatively inexpensive Dutch tiles or spend a fortune on an Old Master. In **Nieuwe Spiegelstraat**, Kunsthandel Aalderink (No. 15) specialises in oriental and ethnographic art; **Staetshuys** (No. 45A) has a good stock of furniture; **Kunsthandel Frans Leidelmeijer** (No. 58) specialises in Art Deco glass, lamps, statues and ceramics; and the **Amsterdam Antiques Gallery** (No. 34) has six dealers under one roof, selling icons, clocks, pewter, paintings and scientific instruments among other things.

The prices are slightly lower in Kerkstraat where **De Haas** (No. 155) specialises in Art Nouveau and Art Deco, and **Lambiek** (No. 78) sells thousands of antique comics and the original drawings of comic artists and cartoonists.

Outside the Spiegelkwartier, **'t Winkeltje** (Prinsengracht 228) is a wonderful jumble of inexpensive antique toys, bottles, lamps, glass and candlesticks.

Books

The Book Exchange (Kloveniersburgwal 42) sells second-hand titles and will accept your unwanted books in part exchange. **Architectura et Natura** (Leliegracht 22) has a comprehensive stock of books in every language on architecture, wildlife and gardening and sometimes mounts exhibitions on the work of the Dutch architectural movements. **Athenaeum** (Spui 14–16) stocks the city's widest range of non-fiction titles. **Jacob van Wijngaarden** (Overtoom 97) is the best for maps and guidebooks to anywhere in the world.

Cakes and Confectionery

Arnold Cornelis (Van Buerkestraat 93) has ravishing window displays and specialises in up-market pâtisserie and handmade chocolates.

Camera Supplies

Foto Professional (Nieuwendijk 113).

Candles

Pontifex (Reestraat 20) sells nothing but candles from all over the world in an extraordinary range of colours and shapes – works of art in wax that you will not want to set alight.

Cheese

Wegewijs Kaas (Rozengracht 32) proves that there is far more to Dutch cheese than Edam and Gouda; **Kef** (Marnixstraat 192) has a superb range of French farmhouse cheeses, and is ideal for picnic supplies since it also sells wine, baguettes, sausages and pâtés.

Chocolates

Hendrikse Le Confiseur (Overtoom 472) makes beautiful chocolates using the finest cocoa. While at **Pompadour** (Huidenstraat 12) you can indulge in rich pastries in the tearoom before buying handmade chocolates, including the truffle specialities.

Cigars and Tobacco

PGC Hajenius (Rokin 92–6) is renowned for its old-world atmosphere, its own brand of cigars and its huge collection of pipes.

Clogs

De Klompenboer (St Antoniesbraestraat 51) makes serious clogs (Klompen) that are meant to be worn, and decorative painted versions for hanging on the wall.

Clothes

Couturiers and boutiques in PC Hooftstraat cater for the moneyed end of the market: **Edgar Vos** (No. 136) sells beautifully tailored clothes for female executives. For more affordable high-street fashions, popular spots are **America Today**, **Magna Plaza shopping mall** (behind Dam square) and Sarphatistraat 48 or **Esprit** (Spui 1c). Cheaper still are shops specialising in vintage or antique garments, such as **Lady Day** (Hartenstraat 9) and **Laura Dols** (Wolvenstraat 7) whose stock includes real collector's items.

Condoms

The **Condomerie het Gulden Vlies** (Warmoesstraat 141) presents its mind-boggling collection with style.

Ethnic Art

Baobab (Elandsgracht 128) sells

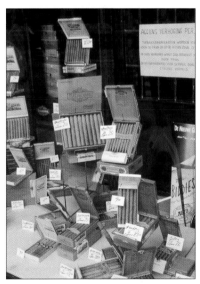

A window for the discerning cigar smoker

Glassware, a decorative memento of Amsterdam

jewellery, furniture and carpets from the Far East.

Fabrics and Trimmings
Capsicum (Oude Hoogstraat 1) specialises in Thai silks and Indian cottons; **Knopen Winkel** (Wolvenstraat 14) in buttons from all over the world; and the **Noordermarkt** (*see p139*) is also an excellent place to buy clothes and fabrics.

Glass and Ceramics
Focke & Meltzer (Binnenhof 59) is a long-established firm selling glass, silver and ceramics from top European producers, and is a showcase for both Delftware and Royal Makkum pottery, still made according to 17th-century glazing techniques.
   The Galleria d'Arte 'Rinascimento' (Prinsengracht 170) specialises in antique and reproduction Delftware and Makkum pottery and the stock ranges from thimbles to tile paintings, tulip vases and apothecaries' jars. **Glasgalerie Kuhler** (Prinsengracht 134) stocks art glass by leading makers at surprisingly reasonable prices.

Herbal Remedies
Jacob Hooy (Kloveniersburgwal 12) sells homeopathic remedies from an original apothecary's shop established in 1743. The stock includes a vast range of culinary herbs and spices, plant-based cosmetics and health foods.

Lace
The genuine article, handmade rather than machine-produced Dutch lace, can be bought at **Het Kantenhuis** (Kalverstraat 124).

Models
The Scale Train House (Bilderdijkstraat

94) sells far more than its name suggests: do-it-yourself construction kits of everything from windmills and three-masted sailing ships to moon-landing craft, as well as a huge stock of railway engines, track and scenery.

Plants

Amsterdam's famous **Bloemenmarkt** (Flower Market) stretches along the Singel Canal from Muntplein to Koningsplein. The 15 florists based here sell a vast range of cut flowers and bulbs. They also sell pot plants; however, check with the stallholders whether the plants you buy are exportable. (*Open: Mon–Sat 9.30am–5.30pm, up to 5pm on Sat.*) Also worth visiting for a range of unusual cut flowers and bouquets are **Maison Riviera** (Herenstraat 2–6) and **Gerda's Bloemenwinkel** (Runstraat 16).

Postcards and Posters

All of Amsterdam's three main museums sell first-class reproductions of the art in their collections. **Art Multiples** (Keizersgracht 510) has an enormous stock from around the world.

Teeth

De Witte Tandenwinkel or The White Teeth Shop (Runstraat 5) is an eccentric but successful outlet for everything to do with dental hygiene; champagne-flavoured toothpaste and novelty tooth-brushes are among the best-selling lines.

Tea and Coffee

Geels en Co (Warmoesstraat 67) products scent the whole street; the shop is a museum of the history of tea and coffee making and historic packaging.

Simon Levelt (Prinsengracht 180) has a vast stock and old tiled interior.

Toys

Beautifully-made toys in wood are a Dutch speciality and many are bought by collectors who have no intention of allowing them to become play-worn. They can be found at **Tesselschade** (Leidseplein 33) and **Pinokkio** (in Masna Plaza, behind Dam Square).

At **Kramer** (Reestraat 18) the owner restores old (and new) dolls and teddy bears.

Videos

Cine-Qua-Non (Staalstraat 14) is a film-lovers' haven, stocking videotapes of cult and art movies that are not widely available on the commercial market, as well as all kinds of posters, magazines, books and memorabilia to do with the cinema.

Tesselschade Toys

Diamonds

Amsterdam has been an important centre for diamond processing since the 17th century. The industry was founded by Jewish refugees who were prohibited from joining the well-established city guilds, which effectively barred them from many areas of employment. They therefore pursued trades which were not regulated – retail trading, banking, printing and diamond working. From these roots the industry blossomed, partly due to the skill of Amsterdam's diamond cutters and polishers, and partly because the Dutch colonies in South Africa proved to be such a rich source of raw diamonds. This led to a boom during the 1870s when diamond processing became the city's fastest-growing sector.

Today Amsterdam's diamond companies concentrate on the jewellery trade since artificial diamonds, invented in the 1950s, are now used for most industrial applications. Several companies offer workshop tours where visitors may learn how rough diamonds are turned into sparkling gems. You will discover the factors that influence the price. These are the four Cs of the diamond trade: the colour (diamonds can be green, blue, rose, yellow or brown as well as pure white), the cut (the number of facets), the clarity (dictated by the number and size of inclusions) and the carat (the weight; 1 carat = 0.2gm). Visitors are also sure to be told about the world's biggest diamond, the Cullinan (found in South Africa, 1905), which weighed 3,106 carats in its rough state: it was cut into 105 separate gems of which the largest, Cullinan I (530 carats), the world's largest cut diamond, occupies pride of place as the central jewel in the British crown.

The following companies give free guided tours on request:

Amsterdam Diamond Centre
Rokin 1–5. Tel: (020) 624 5787; www.amsterdamdiamondcentre.nl. Open: Mon–Wed, Fri–Sat 10am–6pm, Thur 10am–7.30pm, Sun 11am–6pm.

Coster Diamonds
Paulus Potterstraat 2–8. Tel: (020) 305 5555; www.costerdiamonds.com. Open: daily 9am–5pm.

Gassan Diamonds
Nieuwe Uilenburgerstraat 173–5. Tel: (020) 622 5333; www.gassandiamonds.com. Open: daily 9am–5pm.

Stoeltie Diamonds
Wagenstraat 13–17. Tel: (020) 623 7601. Open: daily 9am–5pm.

Van Moppes Diamonds
Albert Cuypstraat 2–6. Tel: (020) 676 1242. Open: daily 9am–5pm.

Diamonds are forever: Amsterdam has been known for perfect diamond processing skills since the 17th century

Entertainment

Amsterdam's lively entertainment scene caters to every taste. At least 14,000 theatrical performances or concerts are said to take place in the city every year, which works out to an average of 40 a day. The VVV Amsterdam Tourist Office publishes a useful monthly listings magazine, *Day by Day*, which specifically concentrates on events that can be enjoyed by English-speaking visitors.

Getting ready to rock in Dam Square

Classical Music, Ballet and Opera
Muziektheater
The Muziektheater is part of the controversial modern Stopera development (*see* Stadhuis *in the* What to See *section, p80*) and it is dogged by poor acoustics; this makes performances by The Netherlands Opera less than perfect, but the problem has been overcome to a degree by the strategic use of hidden microphones. The Dutch National Ballet is also based here and its performances of classics, such as *Swan Lake* and *Sleeping Beauty*, play to capacity audiences, so advance booking is advisable. The Netherlands Dance Theatre puts in occasional guest performances of modern choreography. Musicians from the opera and ballet orchestras give free lunchtime concerts in summer.
Waterlooplein 22. Tel: (020) 625 5455; www.muziektheater.nl
Box office open: Mon–Sun 10am–6pm or

The Muziektheater development

Concertgebouw is filled with the rich sound of masters

*start of performance; Sun 11.30am–6pm
or start of performance.*
Trams: 9 or 14. Metro: Waterlooplein.

Concertgebouw

In contrast to the Muziektheater, the
Concertgebouw is renowned for its
acoustics, which are exploited to the
full by the Royal Concertgebouw
Orchestra, internationally famous for
performances of the big rich works of
Mahler, Strauss, Ravel and Debussy.
In 2004 the orchestra appointed a new
conductor, the Latvian-born Mariss
Jansons. A second smaller hall is used
for chamber works. Concerts are
popular, so advance booking is
advisable.
Concert-gebouwplein 2–6.
Tel: (02) 671 8345; www.concertgebouw.nl

*Box office open: daily 10am–7pm by
phone till 5pm.*
Trams: 3, 5, 12 & 16.

Beurs Van Berlage

Amsterdam's former stock and
commodities exchange is now a cultural
centre, home to The Netherlands
Philharmonic and Chamber Orchestras
who perform in two superbly converted
halls named after the commercial
sponsors, the AGA Zaal and the Wang
Zaal. Concerts cover the whole musical
repertoire and occasionally feature top
international soloists.
*Damrak 277. Tel: (020) 521 7575;
www.berlage.com*
*Box office open: Tue–Fri 2–5pm and two
hours before a performance.*
Trams: 4, 9, 16, 24 & 25.

Churches

The Engelsekkerk (Begijnhof 48; *tel: (020) 624 9665; www.ercadam.nl*) hosts free lunchtime concerts in July and August, and evening concerts throughout the year. Look out for occasional organ recitals and choral concerts in Oude Kerk (Oudekerksplein 23; *tel: (020) 625 8284; www.oudekerk.nl*) and Nieuwe Kerk (Dam Square; *tel: (020) 638 6909; www.nieuwekirk.nl*). The Waalse Kerk (Oudezijds Achterburgwal 157; *tel: (020) 623 2074*) is used for early music recitals and the Ronde Lutherse Kerk (Kattengat 1) hosts occasional Sunday morning recitals.

Muziekgebouw

Opened by the Queen in June 2005, this audaciously modern music centre literally lights up the Docklands area at night. As with most challenging modern buildings, it has both its friends and its critics, but at a cost of €52 million it is hoped that it will succeed in pleasing both the people of Amsterdam and the city's many visitors.

This is no conventional music centre, with an auditorium, a bar and a bookshop. For a start, it has opened its arms and welcomed the city's main jazz club, BimHuis, which has moved here from its former warehouse home. The IJsbreker concert hall cum café, home to many progressive modern works, has also relocated to the Muziekgebouw. The children's KlankSpeelTuin or 'noise playground' is also now under the same roof.

There are temporary exhibitions, conference facilities and a very impressive setting for the restaurant, overlooking the water. Whether the rather disparate collection of activities can settle down and give the Muziekgebouw a distinct identity of its own still remains to be seen. But as a building, it is certainly worth seeing. *Piet Heinkade 1. Tel: (020) 788 2010; www.muziekgebouw.nl Open (for telephone bookings): Mon–Fri 1–5pm. Trams: 16 & 26.*

Café Alto

Legendary jazz bar just off Leidseplein. Small, but big on atmosphere, and with free entry is an inexpensive way to listen to quality modern jazz performed nightly from 10pm to 3am, and often much later. *Korte Leidsedwarsstraat 115. Tel: (020) 626 3249; www.jazz-cafe-alto.nl Open: Sun–Thur 9pm–3am, Fri–Sat 9pm–4am. Trams: 1, 2 & 5.*

Rock Music
Escape

Big, centrally located disco, popular with visitors; live soul and hip-hop bands. *Rembrandtplein 11. Tel: (020) 622 1111; www.escape.nl Open: Thur–Sun from 11pm. Trams: 4, 9 & 14.*

Melkweg

Milky Way – located in an old dairy – was the last bastion of hippiedom until the late 1970s when the building was converted to a modern multimedia centre with a theatre, cinema and concert hall, the latter specialising in world music, reggae, African, Latino and roots music, but also playing host to well-known British and US bands.

Melkweg is run as a cooperative and is informal and relaxed; there is no dress

code, but regulars do turn up in imaginative party dress, especially for the popular Friday and Saturday night discos.
Lijnbaansgracht 234A. Tel: (020) 531 8181; www.melkweg.nl Open: Tue–Sun from 7.30pm. Disco open: Fri–Sat after the live acts, around 1am. Trams: 1, 2, 5, 6, 7 & 10.

Paradiso

This rock venue, converted from a church, offers concerts from big-name bands who love the informal atmosphere and intimacy as a change from the impersonality of huge sports stadium venues. Like its near neighbour Melkweg, world music, reggae, African and Latin music all feature strongly in Paradiso.
Weteringschans 6–8. Tel: (020) 626 4521; www.paradiso.nl Concerts from 8pm on various days; phone for details. Tickets at the door or from the VVV

Amsterdam Tourist Office. Trams: 6, 7 or 10.

Cinema

Almost all films are shown in their original language versions (predominantly English) or with English subtitles; the few exceptions that are only shown in Dutch will feature the words *Nederlands Gesproken* on the poster. Several cinemas mount special afternoon matinees featuring cartoons, science fiction or children's films. Cinema listings are found in numerous bars and cafés and in the free monthly magazine *De Filmkrant* (in Dutch, but easily understood).

Calypso/Bellevue Cinerama

Glitzy two-screen cinema showing the latest popular movies.
Marnixstraat 400. Tel: (020) 623 4876. Trams: 1, 2, 5, 6, 7 & 10.

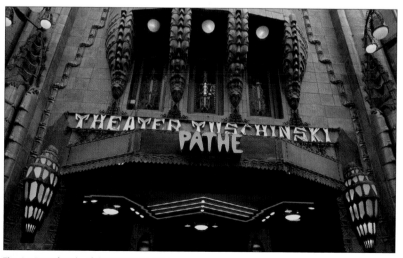

The Art Deco façade of the Tuschinski cinema

The Municipal Theatre by night

City
The biggest cinema in Amsterdam with seven screens; expect to queue at weekends for popular blockbuster movies.
Leidseplein. Tel: (0900) 1458.
Trams: 1, 2, 5, 6, 7 & 10.

Pathé Tuschinski
Worth visiting just for its beautiful and authentic 1920s' interior; Amsterdam's showcase cinema, used for celebrity premières. Expect queues at weekends if you have not booked in advance.
Reguliersbreestraat 26. Tel: (020) 626 2633. Box office open: daily noon–10pm.
Trams: 4, 9 & 14.

The Movies
Neighbourhood cinema specialising in international art movies and classics, with an authentic 1930s' café.
Haarlemmerdijk 161.
Tel: (020) 624 5790. Tram: 3.

De Uitkijk
This small, cosy cinema (near Leidseplein) also presents films for a critical audience.
Prinsengracht 452. Tel: (020) 623 7460.
Trams: 1, 2 & 5.

Nederlands Filmmuseum
The films shown here are drawn from the museum's archives, everything from silent movies (shown with live piano accompaniment) to the art films of Truffaut and Tarkovsky – the whole gamut of European cinema, in fact, and with three different films a day there is plenty of choice. In summer, the terrace of this 19th-century former tea room is used for outdoor screenings.
Vondelpark 3. Tel: (020) 589 1400;
www.filmmuseum.nl Box office open: Mon–Fri 10am–10pm, Sat–Sun 2–10pm. Trams: 1, 2, 3, 5, 6 & 12.

Theatre
Stadsschouwburg
The Municipal Theatre is home to three Dutch theatrical companies which cover mainly the modern, timeless repertoire (Pinter, Albee), and contemporary productions. Until recently, the theatre used to bring English-spoken productions, but at the moment attending a performance is only advisable in June when the theatre is also a venue for Holland Festival (dance) performances.
Leidseplein 26. Tel: (020) 624 2311;
www.ssba.nl Box office open: Mon–Sat 10am–6pm; Sun 1½ hours before performance.
Trams: 1, 2, 5, 6, 7 & 10.

Kleine Komedie

Established in 1786, this is one of Amsterdam's oldest theatres. There are occasional English-language shows, plus performances by the odd pop megastar.

Amstel 56. Tel: (020) 624 0534. Box office open: noon till beginning of show (when performances are on), noon–6pm (when there are no performances). Closed: Sun. Trams: 4, 9, 14, 16, 24 & 25.

Koninklijk Theater Carré

This former circus building is now the venue for big musical and theatrical productions touring from Britain and the USA, and long-standing favourites such as *Cats* and *Les Misérables*. The annual Christmas circus is still a highlight.

Amstel 115–125. Tel: (020) 524 9494; www.theatercarre.nl Box office open: daily 9am–9pm. Trams: 6, 7 & 10.

Open-air Events

On summer Sunday afternoons it can seem that everyone in Amsterdam is heading for **Vondelpark**; the open-air theatre here is used for a very broad range of concerts, from traditional jazz to brass band music and even rock performances by home-grown bands such as The Nits. Between stage acts, there are buskers, jugglers, acrobats and puppeteers to watch. Check what is on at the VVV Amsterdam Tourist Office or just turn up and take pot luck.

Vondelpark: entrance from PC Hooftstraat. Vondelpark Openluchttheater Tel: (020) 673 1499. Trams: 1, 2, 3, 5, 6 & 12.

Colourful modern art in the form of street graffiti decorates a small corner of Vondelpark, a green area renowned for its open-air theatre

Children

Amsterdam is a perfect city for children, who will enjoy canal trips, barrel organs, street buskers and riding the trams as much, if not more, than their parents. Most museums charge lower admission fees for children and will admit infants for free.

Children at play

Favourite children's attractions in the city are the **Madame Tussaud Scenerama** (*see p58*) and the **Van Gogh Museum** (*see pp70–1*). Two museums are specifically aimed at children: the **Kindermuseum** (*see p58*) allows them to learn about life in Africa or the Middle East by exploring implements, clothing, musical instruments and much more. The **NEMO** (*see p59*) is full of push-button models that explain the wonders of holography, lasers, optical illusions, computers and cars. The big attraction for children at the **Nederlands Scheepvaart** (Maritime) **Museum** (*see pp72–3*) is the East Indiaman, the *Amsterdam*, whose narrow passages, staircases and hold can be explored without restriction. The **Aviodome** at Lelystad airport provides the opportunity to play at being pilot in the cockpit of an airliner or to examine a space capsule.

The **Zoo** (Artis, *see p93*) is an absorbing place because it combines so many attractions: there are zoological and geological museums, a planetarium and an aquarium to explore as well as a big collection of wild animals and a smaller corner set up as a children's farm, where the rabbits and goats can be touched and stroked.

Amsterdam has several other children's farms which are not so crowded and which cost nothing to visit (though donations are welcomed). There is one in the Pijp district, **Kinderboerderij De Pijp** (*Lizzy Ansinghstraat 82; tel: (020) 664 8303; open: Mon–Fri 11am–5pm, Sat–Sun 1–5pm*), can be combined with a visit to the nearby NEMO. At the junction of Bickersgracht and Zandhoek, in the Western Islands (*see pp90–1*), you will find the **Dierencapel**, the Animal's Chapel, which is open during daylight hours; children can help with the feeding if they are there at the right time – usually around 4pm.

Parks and Playgrounds
Vondelpark (*see p67 & p151*) is the most central of Amsterdam's green spaces; apart from the playground and the numerous ducks on the lake, there is plenty of free entertainment on summer weekends – acrobats, puppeteers and musicians.
Amsterdamse Bos (*see p130*) can form the focus of a whole day's outing, beginning and ending with a ride on a veteran tram from the **Electrische Museumtramlijn** (*see p47*); the options here include cycling, swimming, boating and horse riding.

Swimming

The **Mirandabad complex** is a great place for burning up energy; the indoor subtropical pool has an artificial beach, water slides, a wave machine and a whirlpool, and there is an outdoor pool as well for summer use.

De Mirandalaan 9. Tel: (020) 546 4444; www.mirandabad.nl
Open: Mon–Fri 7am–10pm, Sat–Sun 10am–5pm. Admission charge.
Tram: 25. Buses: 15, 66 & 199.

Cinema

Children who enjoy films will not be disappointed: several cinemas in Amsterdam have special children's matinées – check with individual cinemas for details.

Theatre

The **Circus Elleboog** may appeal to older children; this is a club which trains children in circus techniques – conjuring, clowning, juggling, unicycle riding and so on – but there are open sessions for all-comers on Saturday afternoons and all day Sunday, and the staff speak English. It is better to book places for your children in advance.

Passeerdersgracht 32. Tel: (020) 626 9370. Admission charge. Trams: 7 & 10.

Babysitters

Babysit Centrale Kriterion is a thoroughly reliable agency employing students who charge very modest rates – hence it is essential to book in advance, especially for weekends (*tel: (020) 697 2320*).

A healthy combination of fun and learning at the Zoo (Artis)

Sport and Leisure

Amsterdammers are not great sports fanatics or fitness freaks, but there are numerous opportunities for working out or taking a relaxing sauna in the city centre. Most of the big sporting events take place outside Amsterdam but the venues are easily reached by public transport or by joining a special coach excursion.

A universal sight, this time in Vondelpark

Health Clubs
A Bigger Splash
An up-market and fashionable fitness centre which has all kinds of facilities including a weights room, exercise gym, Turkish bath, sauna and massage service, as well as aerobics classes throughout the day.
Looiersgracht 26. Tel: (020) 624 8404.
Open: daily 7am–midnight.
Admission charge: a day pass allows free use of all the facilities.
Trams: 7 & 10.

Club Sportive
Luxurious and central establishment with exercise gymnasium and sauna. Aerobics classes for all levels of fitness take place on weekdays at 6 and 7pm and other variable times.
Korte Leidsedwarsstraat 18.
Tel: (020) 620 6631;
www.clubsportive.nl
Open: Mon–Fri 8am–11pm, Sat–Sun 10am–6pm.
Trams: 6, 7, 10, 16, 24 & 25.

Sports Centres
Borchland
Squash, tennis and badminton courts, and indoor bowling green all under one roof.

Borchlandweg 8–12. Tel: (020) 563 3333.
Open: daily 8am–11.30pm (deviations in opening hours are possible).
Admission charge: courts should be booked in advance; higher rates evenings and weekends.
Buses: 59 & 177. Metro: Strandvliet.

Squash
Squash City
Facilities include aerobics, solarium and sauna.
Katelmakerstraat 6. Tel: (020) 626 7883;
www.squashcity.nl Open: from 8.45am daily (Tue–Thur 7am), closes Mon–Thur midnight, Fri 11pm, Sat–Sun 9pm.
Admission charge: higher rates evenings & Sun. Buses: 18 & 22.

Swimming
Marnixbad
Two pools in the brand new Marnix Sports Centre, in the middle of the city.
Marnixstraat 5–9. Tel: (020) 625 4843;
www.marnixbad.nl Open: about to open at the time of this book's publication so ring to check. Admission charge.
Trams: 3 & 10, or bus 18.

Mirandabad
Popular, clean subtropical pool with wave machine, beach, water

slide, whirlpool and outdoor pool in summer.

De Mirandalaan 9.
Tel: (020) 546 4444; www.mirandabad.nl
Open: Mon–Fri 7am–10pm, Sat–Sun 10am–5pm. Admission charge.
Tram: 25. Buses: 15, 66 & 199.

Zuiderbad

This indoor pool was built in 1912. It still retains its tiled period interior and much of the old charm.

Hobbemastraat 26.
Tel: (020) 678 1390.
Open: Mon 7am–9pm, Tue–Fri 7am–10pm, Sat 8am–3.30pm, Sun 10am–3.30pm.
Admission charge
Trams: 1, 2, 5, 16, 24 & 25.

Tennis
Amstelpark

Fifteen indoor and 26 outdoor courts; free racket hire.

Koenenkade 8. Tel: (020) 301 0700;
www.amstelpark.nl Open: daily 8am–11pm or midnight. Hourly court fee.
Buses: 170, 171 & 172.

Watersports
Sloterpark

Watersports centre on the Sloterplas lake with dinghies, windsurfing boards, canoes and wetsuits for hire.

Plantijngracht 4. Tel: (020) 617 5839.
Open: May–Oct, daily 8am–9pm. Hourly hire charge; deposit and identification required. Trams: 1 & 17.

Aquatic fun at the Mirandabad

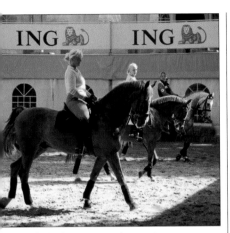

The De Haagse equestrian event

Equestrian Sports

De Haagse Paardendagen, a two-day equestrian event, takes place in Den Haag (The Hague) in the second week in June (details from The Hague VVV Tourist Office, *tel: (0900) 340 3505*). Rotterdam hosts the biggest horse show of the year mid- or end-August (details from the Rotterdam VVV Tourist Office, *tel: (0900) 403 4065*). Amsterdam's own RAI exhibition centre is the venue for Jumping Amsterdam, four days of show-jumping competitions, mostly held end-November (details from the Amsterdam VVV Tourist Office, *tel: (0900) 400 4040*).

Football

Ajax, Amsterdam's home team, reached the peak of its success in the 1970s when it won three European Cup tournaments. Disgrace followed when the team was banned from European competition for a year because of the violent behaviour of its fans, and this was followed by a scandal involving underhand transfer deals.

Under new management the team has experienced a renaissance, winning the UEFA Cup in 1992 and the European Cup again in 1995. The fans are better behaved but matches against traditional rivals Feyenoord of Rotterdam, FC Den Haag, FC Utrecht or PSV Eindhoven are heavily policed as a precautionary measure. Ajax have a new state-of-the-art stadium on the outskirts of the city. It hosts other sporting and entertainment events and has a museum dedicated to Ajax.
Amsterdam ArenA, ArenA Boulevard 1. Tel: (020) 311 1444; www.ajax.nl Tours daily: noon, 2 & 4pm (also 11am Sat–Sun; more tours are offered when there is great interest). Ajax Museum en Fanshop. Tel: (020) 311 1685. Open: daily 9am–5pm. No tours. Museum closed: match days/events. Admission charge.

Golf

The **KLM Open Championship** takes place at the beach resort of Zandvoort, west of Amsterdam, end-July (details from The Dutch Golf Federation; *tel: (030) 662 1888; www.golfsite.nl*).

Hockey

The Wagener Stadium in Amsterdam is the home ground of the city's men's and women's teams and it is also used to stage international competitions.
Nieuwe Kalfjeslaon 19. Tel: (020) 640 1141. Matches: Sept–May, Sun 12.45pm (women), 2.45pm (men). Free admission to league games, admission charge for internationals. Buses: 66, 142, 147, 170, 171 & 172.

Motorsports

The **Zandvoort Circuit**, a short train ride from Amsterdam, is no longer used for Formula 1 racing but there is an exciting choice of international events held every weekend from March to October; details from Esso garages or *tel: (023) 574 0750; www.circuit-zandvoort.nl*

The big event of the year is the International **Netherlands Motorcycling TT Grand Prix**, which is held at Assen end-June. This popular event includes vintage, Formula 1 and sidecar races. Advance booking by post advised.

TT Assen, PO Box 150, 9400 AD Assen. General information: Tel: (0592) 321 321.

Tennis

The **International Tennis Tournament** held in Rotterdam mid-February provides an excellent opportunity to see some of the world's top-seeded players in action.

Information from the Rotterdam Ahoy Hallen. Tel: (0900) 235 2469.

Windsurfing

The challenging conditions of the North Sea make for surfing: contests are held on various dates at Scheveningen, just outside Den Haag. It is a spectacular event.

Details from The Hague VVV Tourist Office. Tel: (0900) 340 3505.

The official museum and fanshop of the Ajax club

Food and Drink

You can eat the food of every nation somewhere, at some spot in Amsterdam. The food ranges from American and Argentinian to Swiss, Thai and Turkish. Amsterdam has literally hundreds of very fine restaurants which serve every kind of cuisine that you would ever have wanted to sample, including some that you have probably never tried, such as Surinamese.

An Argentine restaurant offers its national cuisine

In addition, there are several gourmet shrines – top restaurants that have won Europe-wide acclaim for their inventiveness and quality, most of them French-inspired. These are inevitably expensive, but the majority of the city's restaurants are informal, inexpensive and geared to ordinary wallets.

Amsterdammers themselves do not like pretentiousness in any form and want to relax when they eat out. Restaurateurs have to fit in to survive, hence you will find that children are welcome in most restaurants and that there is nearly always a good vegetarian selection on the menu. Only the most expensive restaurants insist on jacket and tie, otherwise people dress as casually as they please. There is no pressure on diners to buy an expensive bottle of

house wine; most local people prefer a cooling beer or mineral water instead. Another aspect of the easy-going attitude is that few restaurants have non-smoking areas, though the airconditioning usually takes care of the problem and anti-smoking laws are being considered.

There should be no difficulty understanding the menus, which are printed in several languages; waiters will speak English, and often French and German as well. The menu prices include tax (17.5 per cent) and service (15 per cent) so there is no need to worry about hidden extras. Still, it is usual to give a tip, varying between 5 and 10 per cent – but only if you are satisfied with the service. Credit cards are universally accepted. A number of the restaurants listed here are quite small, so it is advisable to book in advance for dinner, especially in summer and at weekends.

The following price indications are based on the cost of a three-course meal per person, excluding the price of drinks:

★ under €20
★★ from €20–25
★★★ from €25–35
★★★★ above €35

A simple breakfast to start the day

African
Kilimanjaro ★★
Small and friendly restaurant with pan-African cuisine – which offers the opportunity to choose dishes from the whole continent.
Rapenburgerplein 6.
Tel: (020) 622 3485.
Open: Tue–Sun 5–10pm.
Trams: 6, 9 & 14.
Tjing Tjing ★★
Specialises in Dutch-South African cuisine from meat to vegan and halal.
Cornelies Troostraat 56–58.
Tel: (020) 676 0923.
Open: Thur–Sun 2pm–late.
Trams: 16, 24 & 25.

Argentinian
Iguazu ★★
One owner comes from Argentina, the other from Brazil, which results in an attractive culinary offer.
Prinsengracht 703.
Tel: (020) 420 3910.
Open: daily 5pm–midnight, Fri & Sat noon–2pm.
Closed: Nov–Mar on Tue.

Caribbean
Rum Runners ★
Young, fun café with tropical decor, renowned for its cocktails. In summer the tables spill out into the garden alongside Westerkerk. Spicy fish stews and cooling salads plus vegetarian options; other dishes seem less distinctively Caribbean and more Tex-Mex in style. Live music Wed–Sun afternoons.
Prinsengracht 277.
Tel: (020) 627 4079.
Open: Mon–Thur 4pm–midnight, Fri–Sun 2pm–2am.
Trams: 13, 14 & 17.

Unwinding at one of the many cafés

Dutch food at its best means, primarily, absolutely fresh fish and seafood served very simply. At its worst it means heavy, calorie-laden food. The watery landscape of The Netherlands produces fresh and saltwater fish in abundance: prized mussels and oysters from the province of Zeeland, eels from the IJsselmeer, herrings and flatfish from the North Sea.

The place to eat fish is **Lucius★★** (*Spuistraat 247; tel: (020) 624 1831; open: daily 5pm–midnight; trams: 1, 2 or 5*). This old-fashioned establishment, with its white-tiled walls and tanks full of fish (not for eating) serves whatever is freshest and in season. The menu is chalked on a blackboard and the ambience is simple; try the *plateau de fruits de mer*.

Two other atmospheric and popular fish restaurants are **Le Pêcheur★★** (*Reguliersdwarsstraat 32. Tel: (020) 624 3121; open: Mon–Fri noon–midnight; Sat–Sun 5pm–midnight; trams: 1, 2, 5 or 11*) and **Sluizer★** (*Utrechtsestraat 43–45; tel: (020) 626 3557; open: daily noon–2.30pm, 5pm–midnight; tram: 4*).

For authentic food, head for the **Hotel Die Port van Cleve ★★** (*Nieuwezijds Voorburgwal 178–180; tel: (020) 624 0047; open: daily noon–10.30pm; trams: 1, 2, 5, 13 or 17*). This venerable institution has two restaurants. The slightly more expensive **Blauwe Parade** is renowned for its interior, covered in old Delftware picture tiles, but for traditional Dutch food you should go to the cheaper **De Poort**. Specialities include split pea soup, (*erwtensoep*) flavoured with bacon, and *hutspot*, a beef and vegetable dish dating back to the Spanish occupation in the mid-16th century. If these do not appeal you can also enjoy steak in both restaurants; millions have been served since the hotel opened its doors in 1870 and every 1,000th steak comes with a complimentary bottle of wine.

For day-to-day Dutch specialities you do not have to eat formally. Fishmongers (*vishandels*) and herring stalls (*haringkarren*) sell tempting lunchtime snacks such as marinated herring, smoked eel, prawns or fresh salmon served in a bread roll. The traditional dish is raw fresh herring, best when the mild-tasting young fish (*nieuwe haring*) is available in spring.

Cafés and sandwich shops (*broodjeszaken*) sell filled rolls or open sandwiches stuffed with cheese, salami, salad and topped with fried eggs (*uitsmijters*). Equally Dutch are the fried food stalls (*frietkramen*) selling delicious chips with mayonnaise or spicy mincemeat balls called *frikadellen*.

When it comes to alcohol, Amsterdammers have a habit of combining their two national drinks – pilsner-style beer and juniper-flavoured gin. The beer is drunk as a chaser to the gin, a combination aptly known as a *kopstoot*, a headbanger. Try gin on its own; *jonge jenever*, young gin, is an aromatic drink often combined with a mixer such as Coca-Cola. Such treatment would be sacrilegious, however, to *oude jenever*, old gin; this mellow, slightly sweet and creamy liquor, sipped ice cold from a traditional stumpy glass, has its own distinctive flavour.

Facing page top: the Dutch love calorie-rich food; bottom: a herring stall
Top: the unique Dutch chips; above: the best way to enjoy a herring

Chinese

Treasure ★★★★

In general, Chinese restaurants offering a range of cuisines are to be avoided on the principle that the Jack of all trades is master of none; this luxurious restaurant is an exception, however, employing specialist master chefs for each of its regional cuisines – Cantonese, Peking and Szechuan – and serving excellent lunchtime dim sum.

Nieuwezijds Voorburgwal 115–117. Tel: (020) 626 0915. Open: daily noon–11pm.

Trams: 1, 2, 5, 13 & 17.

Dynasty ★★★

Very smart and fashionable, with a modern oriental decor of parasols, potted plants, silks and orchids. The food is highly original, based on the Cantonese tradition but combining elements of Thai, Vietnamese and Indonesian cuisine.

Reguliersdwarsstraat 30. Tel: (020) 626 8400. Open: daily 5.30–11pm. Trams: 1, 2 & 5.

Sea Palace ★★★

This floating restaurant, moored in the northern docks, is popular as much

The famed Sea Palace restaurant

for its riverside views and ambience as for its food. Excellent dim sum lunches are served from noon to 3.30pm and the most popular dinner dish is Peking Duck.

Oosterdokskade 8. Tel: (020) 626 4777. Open: daily noon–11pm. Buses: 32, 39 & 43.

Dutch

Bordewijk ★★★★

This restaurant attracts many regular guests and quite rightly so. Food and wines are excellent, the staff is well informed and helpful. It is advisable to book early.

Noordermarkt 7. Tel: (020) 624 3899. Open: Tue–Sun 6.30–10.30pm. Trams: 3 & 10.

Dorrius ★★★

Recently reopened hotel restaurant, but with genuine turn-of-the-20th-century furnishings, decor and signs rediscovered in storage from the time when the former restaurant of the same name closed in the 1890s. Large portions of traditional Dutch food.

Holiday Inn Crowne Plaza, Nieuwezijds Voorburgwal 5. Tel: (020) 420 2224. Open: daily 6–11pm. Trams: 1, 2 & 5.

1e Klas ★★

This café-cum-restaurant used to be Centraal Station's first-class waiting room, and its Art Deco fittings and wood panelling are reminiscent of the golden age of steam trains and cloche hats. The food is modern Dutch (influenced, that is, by French nouvelle cuisine but still rooted in Dutch ingredients and traditions).

Platform 2b, Centraal Station. Tel: (020) 625 0131. Open: daily 8.30am–11pm. Trams: 1, 2, 4, 5, 9, 13, 14, 16, 17, 24 & 25.

De Blonde Hollander ★
One of the few restaurants devoted to typical Dutch food. Many Amsterdammers like to eat in this friendly place. *Leidsekruisstraat 28. Tel: (020) 623 3014. Open: daily 5–10pm. Trams: 1, 2, 5, 6, 7 & 10.*

French

Café Roux ★★★★
The cuisine is supervised by the famous French chef Albert Roux: his presence is noticeable. Nevertheless, the price-quality relation is very reasonable. *Oudezijds Voorburgwal 197. Tel: (020) 555 3560. Open: daily 6.30–10.30am, noon–2.30pm, 3–5pm, 6–10.30pm. Trams: 4, 9, 14, 16, 24 & 25.*

Excelsior ★★★★
Elegant mirrored and chandeliered restaurant with panoramic views over the River Amstel. Seafood and game specialities as well as imaginative vegetarian dishes and a comprehensive wine list.

Hotel de l'Europe, Nieuwe Doelenstraat 2–8. Tel: (020) 531 1705. Open: daily 7–11am and 7–10.30pm, also Mon–Fri 12.30–2.30pm; booking essential; jacket and tie. Trams: 4, 9, 14, 16, 24 & 25.

't Swarte Schaep ★★★★
Alone in a sea of fast-food outlets, the Black Sheep maintains the highest culinary standards while remaining relatively inexpensive. Even members of the Dutch royal family come here for the subtle blend of traditional French and Dutch cuisine, and characterful timbered interior of the 300-year-old building. *Korte Leidsedwarsstraat 24. Tel: (020) 622 3021. Open: daily noon–11pm; booking advised. Trams: 1, 2 & 5.*

De Gouden Reael ★★★
Former café in the characterful Western Islands (*see* Unknown Amsterdam, *p91*) specialising in regional French cuisine, served with friendliness and flair. Inexpensive set menus. *Zandhoek 14, Westerdok. Tel: (020) 623 3883. Open: Mon–Fri noon–2pm, Sat & Sun also 6–10pm. Tram: 3.*

D' Vijff Vlieghen ★★★
The Five Flies is rather dismissively described by Amsterdammers as a tourist trap but do not be deterred; the cooking is a blend of Dutch and French but the ambience is the main attraction – tables are set in intimate corners of an old house full of period furniture and antiques, lit by candles to create a romantic atmosphere.

Irresistible fruit pastries

Spuistraat 294–302.
Tel: (020) 624 8369.
Open: daily 5.30–
10.30pm. Trams: 1, 2 & 5.
Van Vlaanderen ★★★
Among connoisseurs,
this charming and
unpretentious restaurant
was known already for its
adventurous and refined
cooking. Recognition
from official quarters has
followed: recently, Van
Vlaanderen was awarded
with a Michelin star.
Weteringschans 175.
Tel: (020) 622 8292.

Open: Tue–Sat 6.30–
10.30pm. Closed: Sun &
Mon. Trams: 6, 7, 10, 16,
24 & 25.

Greek
Aphrodite ★
Inexpensive, friendly and
authentic Greek
restaurant. Try the *mezes*,
a multi-course set menu,
for a real feast.
Lange Leidsedwarsstraat
91. Tel: (020) 622 7382.
Open: daily 5pm–
midnight. Trams: 1, 2, 5,
6, 7 & 10.

Café with a streetside view

Indian
Koh-I-Noor ★★
Popular restaurant
serving all the classic
northern Indian dishes
plus inexpensive meat
and vegetarian *thali* set
menus.
Westermarkt 29.
Tel: (020) 623 3133. Also
at Rokin 18, tel: (020) 627
2118. Open: daily 5pm–
midnight, Sun also noon–
3pm. Trams: 13, 14 & 17.
Mayur ★
One of the best Indian
restaurants in
Amsterdam, specialising
in tandoori dishes.
Friendly service.
Korte Leidsedwarsstraat
203. Tel: (020) 623 2142.
Open: daily 5–11.30pm.
Trams: 1, 2, 5, 6, 7 & 10.
The Tandoor ★
An Amsterdam
institution, the first
Indian restaurant in the
city and still popular for
inexpensive tandoori
dishes, plus views over
the busy nightlife of
Leidseplein.
Leidseplein 19.
Tel: (020) 623 4415.
Open: daily 5–11pm.
Trams: 1, 2, 5, 6, 7 & 10.

Indonesian
Amsterdam has
numerous Indonesian
restaurants, thanks to its

colonial legacy, and Amsterdammers love this spicy cuisine as the antithesis to their own bland cooking. By far the majority of the restaurants serve a hybrid mixture of Indo-Chinese food, often further modified to appeal to Dutch taste. Far more authentic are the specialist restaurants listed below, often family-run and serving traditional regional dishes. Most offer a range of *rijsttafels* – set menus consisting of 15 to 45 different dishes served with rice and a fiery chilli sauce called *sambal*, best treated with caution. A simple *rijsttafel* of 15 dishes will provide a remarkably cheap meal of varying flavours and textures, while the more expensive versions usually feature a greater range of meat dishes – *saté*, beef *randang*, suckling pig, sweet and sour pork and mild curried chicken are typical.

Kantjil en de Tijger ★★★
The authentic Indonesian cuisine of this spacious restaurant offers a wide range of dishes. A *rijsttafel* (rice table) is the best way to make acquaintance with the ability of the cooks.
Spuistraat 291–293.
Tel: (020) 620 0994.
Open: daily 4.30–11pm.
Trams: 1, 2 & 5.

Tempo Doeloe ★★★
The cuisine of this renowned restaurant is from the island of Celebes, where the residents favour hot dishes. Luckily, these dishes are clearly indicated on the menu and there are also milder dishes.
Utrechtsestraat 75.
Tel: (020) 625 6718.
Open: daily 6–11.30pm.
Trams: 4, 9 & 14.

Cilubang ★/★★
One of Amsterdam's best small Indonesian restaurants, a quiet and relaxing hideaway.
Runstraat 10.
Tel: (020) 626 9755.
Open: Tue–Sun 5–11pm.
Trams: 1, 2, 5, 7 & 10.

Indonesia ★/★★
Large restaurant specialising in Balinese cuisine with elegant decor, waiters in traditional dress and taped *gamalan* music in the background.
Korte Leidsedwarsstraat 18. Tel: (020) 623 2035.
Open: 5–11pm.
Trams: 1, 2, 5, 6, 7 & 10.

Indonesian restaurant Cilubang

Sama Sebo ★★
Some of the best Indonesian food in Amsterdam. The first evening sitting (6pm) is popular with people going to the theatre or the Concertgebouw but is best avoided in favour of the second sitting (8pm) if you want to linger over your meal.
PC Hooftstraat 27.
Tel: (020) 662 8146.
Open: Mon–Sat noon–2pm, 6–10pm; booking essential.
Trams: 2, 3, 5 & 12.

Viva Mexico!

Irish
The Tara ★
Irish breakfasts and other dishes, with music at night. *Rokin 85–89. Tel: (020) 421 2654. Open: food from 11am–9pm daily. Trams: 4, 9, 14, 16, 24 & 25.*

Italian
Segugio ★★★★
Culinary reviewers wrote praisingly on the achievements of this recently opened restaurant. This makes it obligatory to make a reservation well in advance. *Utrechtsestraat 96. Tel: (020) 330 1503. Open: daily 6–11pm. Trams: 4, 9 & 14.*

Ristorante Caruso ★★
Spacious and stylishly furnished restaurant. Serves classic dishes. *Singel 550. Tel: (020) 623 8320. Open: daily from 8.30pm. Trams: 4, 9, 14, 16, 20, 24 & 25.*
Pizzeria Mimo ★
Authentic and lively pizzeria near Leidseplein. *Lange Leidsedwarsstraat 37. Tel: (020) 622 7935. Trams: 1, 2 & 5.*

Japanese
Sazanka Teppan Yaki/Yamazato ★★★
Two restaurants staffed by Japanese chefs who perform publicly with enormous style and confidence, using ingredients flown in fresh from Japan daily. Lunch menus reasonably priced. *Hotel Okura, Ferdinand Bolstraat 333. Tel: (020) 678 7450/678 7111. Sazanka Teppan Yaki open: daily 6.30–10pm, Mon–Fri noon–2pm. Jacket and tie required. Yamazato open: daily 7.30–9.30am, noon–2pm, 6–9.30pm. Tram: 12.*

Mexican
Pacifico ★★
Offshoot of London's Café Pacifico, with similar decor, but smaller and packed at weekends. Authentic flavours washed down by margaritas (visit on Tuesday night for cut-price drinks and Thursdays for ribs – one price for all you can eat). *Warmoesstraat 31. Tel: (020) 624 2911. Open: Mon–Thur & Sun 5.30–10pm, Fri–Sat 5.30–11pm. Booking advisable. Trams: 4, 9, 14, 16, 20, 24 & 25.*

Spanish
Centra ★
Authentic *tapas*, paella and *zarzuela* (fish stew) and a good choice of Spanish wines. *Lange Niezel 29. Tel: (020) 622 3050. Open: daily 1.30–11pm. Trams: 4, 9, 16, 24 & 25.*

Surinamese
Marowijne ★
Neighbourhood restaurant favoured by local Surinamese, a good place to try this hybrid cuisine which combines Indonesian-influenced dishes (introduced by Dutch civil servants) based on rice and noodles, with South American dishes based on cassava and coconut.

Albert Cuypstraat 68–70.
Tel: (020) 662 4845.
Open: daily noon–10pm.
Trams: 16, 24 & 25.

Swiss

Bern ★
Simple brown café
specialising in fondue and
peppered steaks.
Nieuwmarkt 9.
Tel: (020) 622 0034.
Open: daily 4pm–1am.
Metro: Nieuwmarkt.

Thai

Lana Thai ★★★
The best in town, with a
comprehensive menu.
Warmoesstraat 10.
Tel: (020) 624 2179.
Open: Wed–Mon
5–11.30pm. Trams: 4, 9,
16, 24 & 25.

Vegetarian
All the restaurants listed
above serve vegetarian
dishes, either as part of
the menu or on request.
If, however, you have
special dietary preferences,
try one of the following.

De Bolhoed ★
Hearty organic and
vegan dishes. Excellent
value set-price menu
that changes daily.
Renowned for pastries
and banana-cream pie.
Prinsengracht 60.
Tel: (020) 626 1803.

Open: daily noon–10pm.
Trams: 13, 14 & 17.

De Waaghals ★
Organically produced
food and wine and vegan
dishes. Other dietary
requirements catered for if
you phone in advance.

Frans Halsstraat 29.
Tel: (020) 679 9609.
Open: Tue–Sun 5–9.30pm.
No credit cards.
No-smoking area.
Trams: 16, 24 & 25.

One of the more popular open-air restaurants in Amsterdam

Brown Cafés

The *bruine kroegen*, or brown cafés, of Amsterdam are a uniquely Dutch institution. The typical features are wood-panelled walls and coffee-coloured ceilings, looking as if they had been stained by centuries of tobacco smoke. The wooden tables are sometimes covered in faded Persian rugs to soak up the spilt beer. Brown cafés are an alternative living room, home from home for the regular clientele, a warm place of refuge in winter when the big, pot-bellied stoves are lit and glowing, and the focus of much community activity. People come here for breakfast, morning coffee or an inexpensive lunch, to relax after work, read the paper, play chess, snooker or draughts, or just to chat with their friends.

Brown cafés are found on every street corner, but many of the most characterful are in the Jordaan district. **Café 't Smalle** (*Egelantiers-gracht 12; trams: 3, 10, 13, 14 or 17*) is one of the oldest, originally founded in 1780 as the outlet of a gin distillery. It retains its 18th-century interior and stained-glass windows and serves spicy Dutch apple cake to help soak up the beer.

On Spui (*trams: 1, 2, 4, 5, 9, 14, 16, 24 or 25*) you will find two very popular cafés next to each other. **Café Hoppe** (*Spui 18–20*), with its sawdust-covered floor, was founded in 1670 and is now very popular with trendy business executives, while **Luxembourg** (*Spui 22*) is a café in the grand style. Their distinctions are often blurred in summer when the cafés spill out on to the sunny pavements to form one happy throng.

A variation on the brown café is the *proeflokaal*, or tasting house, where you can sample a very wide range of different beers, wines, gins, or liqueurs. One of the most atmospheric is **Wijnand Fockink**, tucked away off Dam Square at Pijlsteeg 31 (*trams: 4, 9, 14, 16, 24 or 25*). Another is **de Wildeman** (*Kolksteeg 3; trams: 1, 2, 4, 9, 13, 14, 16, 17, 24 or 25*) which always has 18 draught beers on tap, and 200 bottled ales.

   A more recent phenomenon is the so-called white café – designer bars with high-tech interiors – such as **De Jaren** (*Nieuwe Doelenstraat 20; trams: 4, 9, 14, 16, 17, 24 or 25*). White is, however, too clinical a colour for the taste of many Amsterdammers who only feel really at home surrounded by the mellow patina of aged wood and the golden colours of a Rembrandt painting.

Brown cafés have an atmosphere of their own as does the Proeflokaal, or tasting house (below)
Facing page above: a welcome sign for beer-drinkers

Hotels and Accommodation

Although Amsterdam has a great number of hotels, it is also a popular tourist destination and has a thriving conference trade so advance booking is essential in the busiest seasons – Christmas and New Year, Easter and from the beginning of the bulb season in late March to the end of summer, mid-September.

The Golden Tulip Barbizon Palace

One of the simplest ways to book accommodation is to use the **Netherlands Reservation Centre**, or Nederlands Reserverings Centrum (Nieuwe Gouw 1, 1442 LE, Purmerend; *tel: (0299) 689 144; fax: (0299) 689 154; www.hotelres.nl*). Reservations can be

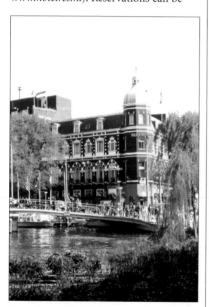

The welcoming Park Hotel

made in writing, by telephone or fax – no personal callers. This free service covers the whole of the country and will save numerous potentially fruitless phone calls to individual hotels. Hotels in The Netherlands are graded according to a star system, from the cheapest one-star establishments to five-star elegance. As with all such systems, the classification is a useful guide to price and facilities but tells you nothing about the character of the hotels and their owners.

In Amsterdam, the choice essentially falls into three categories: canalside hotels (price range from €135 to €185 for a double bedroom), family-run hotels (price range from €100 to €150) and larger establishments (€165 upwards). For most visitors, the idea of a centrally located hotel within the canal circle is very appealing. The main drawback is that these buildings are often protected monuments so the owners cannot simply install lifts, enlarge the rooms or put in modern facilities at will. Rooms may be small and the staircases are often as steep as ladders, so the less-mobile visitor will have real problems. On the plus side, many canalside hotels have attractive gardens and retain characterful period details, redolent of the Golden Age; their proud owners also ensure that the rooms are appropriately furnished with antiques. There are also many elegant purpose-built hotels in the Dam Square and station area which combine the benefits of centrality with a much greater range of facilities.

Most of the family-run hotels in Amsterdam are located in the Museum Quarter and Vondelpark district. Visitors must be sure to check the precise location before booking; do not trust descriptions that say '10 minutes from the centre'.

Hotels in the streets immediately around the three big museums make an ideal base, but the further out you go into the Vondelpark district, the more remote you are from public transport and the further it is to walk to the main sights of interest.

Family-run hotels offer clean basic accommodation at reasonable prices. As with all but the most expensive hotels, breakfast is included in the room price, but too many hotels serve an unappetising buffet of processed cheese, cheap cooked meats, tasteless bread and lukewarm tea or coffee. Any hotel that offers a better choice is to be preferred.

The larger hotel establishments dot the city, and they range from palatial Empire-style buildings with grand staircases and spacious balconied rooms to ultra-modern buildings with waterfalls, art galleries and huge atriums. They all have the facilities you would expect of an international-class

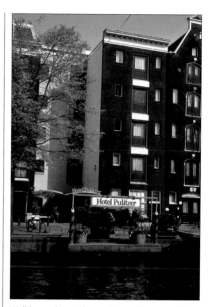

Well located near the centre, on the canalside

hotel – business centres, pools and fitness centres, shopping, valet parking and hairdressers.

If you are visiting Amsterdam on business, it may be worth sacrificing a central location for the greater convenience of a modern hotel on the edge of the city. The problems of driving and parking in Amsterdam are such that busy business executives do not like coming into the centre if they can avoid it. Most industries are located on the southern periphery and some of the best hotels are to be found in the same area, close to the RAI exhibition centre and World Trade Centre. Your Dutch counterparts will thank you for choosing a hotel where they can park easily, and you are only a short taxi ride from the nightlife of the city centre.

Practical Guide

Arriving
Passports

All visitors must have a valid passport to visit The Netherlands for up to three months but visas are needed by some countries, so check before travelling. Citizens of the EU, USA, Canada, Australia and NZ do not need visas.

Getting There

Amsterdam is easily reached by ferry from the United Kingdom, by train from continental Europe or from the UK via the Channel Tunnel and by road from western Germany, Belgium and northern France. Even so, most visitors arrive by air, flying into Amsterdam Schiphol Airport, located 14km southwest of the city centre. This is one of the world's best and busiest airports, served by direct flights from most other international airports. Competition on these routes is such that you can nearly always find a cheap flight if you book far enough in advance and travel midweek.

Airport Facilities

Schiphol is very efficient and you should clear the airport within 20 to 30 minutes of landing. There is a bureau de change in the arrivals hall as well as duty-free shopping, an accommodation booking desk and car rental facilities.

City Link

The entrance to Schiphol station is close to the customs exit and tickets can be bought in the main hall. Trains depart several times an hour between 5.40–1am and at hourly intervals in between. The fare is low and the journey takes 20 minutes. Catch a train for Amsterdam CS (Centraal Station) if you are staying in the city centre. Board trains for Amsterdam Zuid/WTC or Amsterdam RAI only if you are staying in the World Trade Centre/RAI exhibition centre district in the southern suburbs. On arrival it is best to take a taxi from the station to the hotel until you have gained your bearings.

Departing

Confirm your flight with the issuing airline 72 hours before departure (airline telephone numbers are listed in the *Amsterdam Yellow Pages*, or *Gouden Gids* directory). Check-in time at Schiphol is at least one-and-a-half hours before the scheduled flight time. There are excellent shopping and duty-free facilities at the airport – seeds, bulbs and floral bouquets are popular purchases but some countries do not allow the import of plant material; the knowledgeable florists will advise you.

By Train, Ferry or Coach

There are good, fast rail connections to Amsterdam from Brussels, Paris, Antwerp and Cologne, and from London (Eurostar – via the Channel Tunnel; change at Brussels). From London, boat/train services operate from Liverpool Street station via Harwich and the Hook of Holland. Ferry companies in the UK offer services from Harwich to the Hook of Holland, from Hull to Rotterdam and from Newcastle to IJmuiden, with train (bus rom IJmuiden) connections from each erry terminal to Amsterdam. Coach ervices depart from London's Victoria oach terminal. Details of all these ervices are available from travel agents nd rail travel centres but remember hat the journey time can be anything rom 7 to 15 hours and that it is often ust as cheap to fly. The *Thomas Cook uropean Timetable* has details of these ail and ferry services, including night rains, and is available from Thomas ook branches in the UK or by elephoning *00 44 1733 416477.*

amping
he best-equipped and most central ampsite is located on the southern edge f the Amsterdamse Bos, at Kleine loordijk 1 (*tel: (020) 641 6868; ww.campingamsterdamsebos.nl*) and is open from April to October. Using bus 171, it is a 30-minute journey to the city centre. Facilities include telephones, a shop, restaurant and bar, bicycles for hire, log cabins for rent and a lake for swimming.

Children
Children are generally welcomed and indulged. Many restaurants offer children's menus or children's portions at reduced prices. Children also pay reduced fares on public transport. Museums admit infants for free and, as a rule, children under 16 are admitted half price. Several museums offer discounted family tickets (two children and two adults), but the best deal for anyone planning to visit several museums is the Amsterdam Pass (*see p180*).

msterdam Schiphol Airport

Climate

Amsterdam has a maritime climate so it rarely suffers temperature extremes. It is cold enough to freeze the canals only once in every 10 to 15 years, though it can seem cold in winter because strong winds increase the chill factor, and fog blots out the sunlight for days. Summer temperatures average 22°C/72°F, but it may be warmer during the day; the nights are often cool enough to make a light sweater necessary. Prolonged heavy rain is a problem only in November, February and March.

Conversion Tables

See p175.
Amsterdam follows the Rest of Europe system in clothes and shoe sizes.

Crime

Amsterdam's crime problem has been greatly exaggerated, but even so, it is

Possessions should be made safe and secure

AMSTERDAM

July–November

May–August

Weather Conversion Chart
25.4mm = 1 inch
°F = 1.8 x °C + 32

essential to take precautions – most victims of crime invite trouble by carelessness or ill-advised behaviour. Highly organised teams of pickpockets, mainly from North Africa and South America, operate in summer, preying on tourists. Leave valuables in the hotel safe and if you must carry them, conceal them in a body belt or something similar and keep a tight hold on your camera.

Be especially wary in crowded shopping streets or on public transport (the trains between Amsterdam and Schiphol are notorious). Beware of anyone who approaches you, no matter how harmless their enquiry; they may be distracting you while an accomplice goes to work. You should also be careful when giving money to buskers or beggars; there are people about watching to see where you keep your money.

After pickpocketing, car theft is the biggest category of crime. Never leave valuables in the car.

Mugging is less of a problem, but do not go out alone after dark anywhere where drug addicts, desperate for a fix, could attack you unseen; avoid parks, unlit and empty streets and the red-light district – and never try to take photographs in the red-light district; your camera could end up in the canal. If you are the victim of crime, you should file a statement with the nearest police station; it is unlikely that your property will be recovered, but you need an officially stamped copy of the statement to make an insurance claim.

Report the loss of your passport to your embassy or consulate (*see* pp178–9*).* Lost or stolen credit cards can be reported on the following 24-hour lines:

Eurocard/MasterCard
Tel: (030) 283 5555.
American Express *Tel: (020) 504 8666.*
Diners Club *Tel: (020) 654 5511.*
VISA *Tel: (020) 660 0600/660 0611.*

Customs Regulations

Personal possessions are not liable to duty but it is forbidden to import drugs, firearms or weapons (including knives). The current duty-free limits for the import of alcohol, tobacco, perfume and cologne are posted at airports and ferry terminals.

The allowances for importing goods duty- and tax-paid from other European Union nations are very generous.

Conversion Table

FROM	TO	MULTIPLY BY
Inches	Centimetres	2.54
Feet	Metres	0.3048
Yards	Metres	0.9144
Miles	Kilometres	1.6090
Acres	Hectares	0.4047
Gallons	Litres	4.5460
Ounces	Grams	28.35
Pounds	Grams	453.6
Pounds	Kilograms	0.4536
Tons	Tonnes	1.0160

To convert back, for example from centimetres to inches, divide by the number in the third column.

Men's Suits

UK		36	38	40	42	44	46	48
Rest of Europe	46	48	50	52	54	56	58
USA		36	38	40	42	44	46	48

Dress Sizes

UK		8	10	12	14	16	18
France	36	38	40	42	44	46
Italy	38	40	42	44	46	48
Rest of Europe	34	36	38	40	42	44
USA	6	8	10	12	14	16

Men's Shirts

UK	14	14.5	15	15.5	16	16.5	17
Rest of Europe	36	37	38	39/40	41	42	43
USA	14	14.5	15	15.5	16	16.5	17

Men's Shoes

UK	7	7.5	8.5		9.5	10.5	11
Rest of Europe	41	42	43	44	45	46
USA	8	8.5	9.5	10.5	11.5	12

Women's Shoes

UK		4.5	5	5.5	6	6.5	7
Rest of Europe	38	38	39	39	40	41
USA	6	6.5	7	7.5	8	8.5

Stricter limits apply to goods bought in duty-free shops.

Cycling

Cycling in Amsterdam takes practice and courage, and the excellent tram system offers a far easier way of getting around. You may, however, wish to escape the city and explore nearby nature reserves (*see* Cycle Routes *on pp132–3*), and one of the easiest ways of doing that is to rent a bike and move out. These are the main places from where you can rent a bike in Amsterdam:

Bike City
Bloemgracht 68. Tel: (020) 626 3721.

Damstraat Rent a Bike
Damstraat 20-22. Tel: (020) 625 5029.
Holland Rent A Bike
Damrak 247. Tel: (020) 622 3207.
MacBike
Mr Visserplein 2. Tel: (020) 620 0985.
Weteringschans 2–4. Tel: (020) 620 0985.
Stationsplein 12. Tel: (020) 620 0985;
www.macbike.nl

To hire a bike you need to leave a deposit and show your passport or a credit card. It is best to hire a bike with conventional brakes and gearing: old-fashioned Dutch bikes have no gears or hand brakes and are stopped by back pedalling.

Cycling is safe and a common mode of transport both in the city and the countryside

You will be given advice on how to avoid theft of the bike, which you would be wise to heed. You will then have to cope with chaotic traffic and the wayward behaviour of pedestrians and other cyclists. Here is a tip: dismount at busy junctions and cross on foot until you have mastered the basic traffic rules.

Driving

Driving in Amsterdam is not recommended. The city already has too many cars, parking is difficult and cars are a favourite target of thieves. Instead, park your car outside the city centre and use public transport.

If you do drive to Amsterdam, choose a hotel with secure parking and leave your vehicle there for the duration of your stay.

Breakdown

If you are a member of an AIT-affiliated motoring association, you can use the services of the ANWB (Royal Dutch Touring Club) for free on production of an AIT Assistance Booklet (or ETI Booklet). For the emergency breakdown service, you can call from yellow roadside booths along major roads: *tel: 0800 0888.*

If you are not covered by this scheme it might be worth joining the ANWB for the duration of your stay. You may contact the ANWB at Museumplein 5 or call *tel: (020) 673 0844; open: Mon–Fri 9.30am–6pm, Sat 9.30am–5pm.*

Car Rental

Drivers who are more than 21 years old and have at least a year's driving experience can hire a car on production

Trams are part of the landscape

of a valid licence, passport and credit card. The main rental agencies (*auto verhuur*) all have offices at Schiphol airport and at these city-centre addresses:

Avis *Nassaukade 380.*
Tel: (020) 683 6061.
Budget Rent a Car *Overtoom 121.*
Tel: (020) 612 6066.
Europcar *Overtoom 197.*
Tel: (020) 683 2123.
Hertz *Overtoom 333.*
Tel: (020) 612 2441.

Slightly less expensive are the following local firms:

Adams *Nassaukade 346.*
Tel: (020) 685 0111.
Amcar *Jacob Obrechtplein 13–15.*
Tel: (020) 662 4214.
Kuperus *Middenweg 175.*
Tel: (020) 693 8790.
Chauffeur-Driven Cars
CS Limousine Service *Emmastraat 32.*
Tel: (020) 673 7888.
Van Delden Limousine Service
Visseringstraat 21–3.
Tel: (020) 684 8408.

Documents

To enter The Netherlands with a car, you must carry the vehicle registration documents, proof of insurance (such as a Green Card), proof that the vehicle is roadworthy (an MOT certificate) and your driving licence. You must also affix an international identification disc to the rear of the car. If you belong to a motoring organisation, bring your AIT Assistance Booklet (or ETI Booklet) to make use of the AWNB breakdown services for free (*see* **Breakdown**).

Rules of the Road

Traffic drives on the right. Front seatbelts must be worn, and rear seatbelts if fitted. It is illegal to drive after drinking any alcohol. Maximum speeds are 120kph or 100kph on motorways (*autosnelweg*), 80kph on main roads and 50kph in built-up areas. Many residential areas have adopted traffic-calming schemes and laid down 'sleeping policemen' – raised ridges in the road identified by a sign showing a white house against a blue background –

and in these zones it is illegal to drive faster than walking pace.

Parking

Apart from hotels, there is secure parking at Europarking (*Marnixstraat 250; tel: (020) 623 6694*) and metered parking along the banks of the main canals – but space is difficult to find during office hours. Your car is likely to be clamped if you outstay the allotted time shown on the meter; the ticket affixed to the window will explain where and how to pay your fine. Cars parked illegally or dangerously are taken to the police car pound, and released only after payment of a substantial fine in cash.

Petrol

Only unleaded petrol is available in the Netherlands. However, 98-octane Super (not Super Plus) contains an additive, making it suitable for vehicles designed to run on leaded petrol.

Electricity

220 volts, continental 2-pin round style plugs. Non-continental appliances need an adaptor; appliances running on less than 220 volts need a transformer.

Embassies and Consulates

Most are located in Den Haag (The Hague); a comprehensive listing is given in the *Amsterdam Yellow Pages* directory.
Australia *Carnegielaan 4, Den Haag.*
Tel: (070) 310 8200.
Canada *Sophialaan 7, Den Haag.*
Tel: (070) 311 1600.

Ireland *Dr Kuyperstraat 9, Den Haag.*
Tel: (070) 363 0993.
New Zealand *Carnegielaan 10,*
Den Haag. Tel: (070) 365 8037.
UK *Koningslaan 44.*
Tel: (020) 676 4343.
USA *Museumplein 19.*
Tel: (020) 575 5309.

Emergency Telephone Numbers
Police, **Fire and Ambulance** *112.*

Health
If you need medical or dental treatment,
call the Tourist Medical Service on *(020)*
592 3434. This 24-hour line is
specifically geared to visitors and will
refer you to an appropriate doctor,
dentist, pharmacy or hospital.

All EU countries have reciprocal
arrangements for reclaiming the cost of
medical services. UK residents should
obtain the European Health Insurance
Card from any UK post office. However,
10 per cent of the cost of prescribed
medicines and all dental treatment must
be paid for. Travel insurance that
includes medical costs is still advised
and is essential for non-EU nationals.

Language
English is rapidly becoming the first
language of Amsterdam and virtually
everyone speaks it fluently. Signs are
written in English and Dutch, and
menus are printed in several languages,
so communication is rarely a problem.

Lost Property
For items lost on trains: **NS Lost
Property Information** (*tel: (0900) 202
1163*; open: Mon–Fri 8am–8pm, Sat

8am–5pm). Items are kept for three
days, then forwarded to a central depot
in Utrecht.

For items lost on the bus, tram or
Metro system: **GVB Lost Property**
(*Prins Hendrikkade 108–14;*
tel: (0900) 8011; open: Mon–Fri
9am–4.30pm).

Otherwise try **Police Lost Property**
(*Stephensonstraat 18; tel: (020) 559 3005;*
open: Mon–Fri 9.30am–3.30pm).

Maps
Falkplan publishes a series of
comprehensive and up-to-date maps in
various formats: foldout, pocket book,
and a 'patent folded' version which is
almost impossible to use in windy
weather. These and other maps can be
purchased at bookshops and the VVV
Tourist Information Office.

Street graffiti

Media

If your hotel is linked into the cable network you can watch a wide range of TV programmes from all over Europe, including BBC1 and BBC2, French, German, Belgian and Italian stations, children's channels, non-stop pop videos and American news channels.

Cable radio supplies BBC Radio 4, BBC World Service and Voice of America. Foreign newspapers and magazines are widely available on the day of publication.

Money Matters

The Dutch unit of currency is the euro, written as €. The Netherlands shares the new currency with eleven European Union countries: Austria, Belgium, Finland, France, Germany, Greece, Ireland, Italy, Luxembourg, Portugal and Spain. Notes come in denominations of 5, 10, 20, 50, 100, 200 or 500 euros. The euro is subdivided into 100 cents. Coins come in values of 1, 2, 5, 10, 20 and 50 cents, and 1 and 2 euro.

Credit cards are accepted just about everywhere for higher value purchases, as are traveller's cheques and Eurocheques.

Money can be changed at banks and post offices. Amsterdam also has scores of bureaux de change around Dam Square and along Damrak. Some include a substantial commission. Hotels give you a poor rate.

Value Added Tax

BTW tax of 17.5 per cent is included in the price of most retail goods; so if you are a resident of a country outside the EU it makes sense to take advantage of the Tax-free for Tourists scheme when you make high-value purchases. All participating retailers will give you details of how to obtain a refund.

Museum and Leisure Discounts

Visitors will save a lot of money by investing in an Amsterdam Pass. It includes free admission to more than 20 museums and attractions, the use of public transport and one free canal tour and 25 per cent discounts in many other attractions and restaurants. The holder will receive a free brochure which contains the details.

The pass is available from the VVV Amsterdam Tourist Office or Holland Tourist Information at Schiphol airport or ask at your hotel.

National Holidays

Businesses and shops are closed on the following days – although many shops now stay open on Good Friday. Museums are open, but for shorter hours, except on Christmas Day and New Year's Day.

1 January New Year's Day
March/April Good Friday
March/April Easter Monday
30 April Queen's Birthday
Variable Ascension Day
Variable Whit Monday
25 December Christmas Day
26 December Boxing Day.

Opening Hours

Banks Normally open Monday to Friday 9am to 4/5pm; some stay open until 7pm on Thursday and open on Saturday. The GWK Bank in Amsterdam Centraal Station never closes.

Shops Most shops are open from 9am to 6pm (5pm on Saturday), though they may, if they wish, stay open until 10pm. There is late-night opening until 9pm on Thursday. Shops stay closed on Monday until 1pm (department stores 11am). Many shops also open Sunday, usually from noon to 5pm.

Organised Tours
Boat Tours
Touring the canals of Amsterdam by boat is a must for a different perspective on the city. Tour operators usually supply taped commentaries in several languages to point out the various landmarks along the route.

Day cruises last around an hour and there are more expensive lunch and dinner cruises, at which food is served, lasting up to three hours. Day cruises depart at roughly 30-minute intervals from 9am to 6pm daily (services may be restricted in winter).

Reservations are required for lunch and dinner cruises, but even without bookings, you could just turn up at the landing stage. The main operators are:

Canal Cruises
Stadhouderskade 25. Tel: (020) 679 1370; www.canal-cruises.nl

Holland International
Prins Hendrikkade 33a. Tel: (020) 622 7788.

Lovers
Opposite Prins Hendrikkade 25–7. Tel: (020) 530 1090; www.lovers.nl

Meyer
Damrak, moorings 4 and 5. Tel: (020) 623 4208.

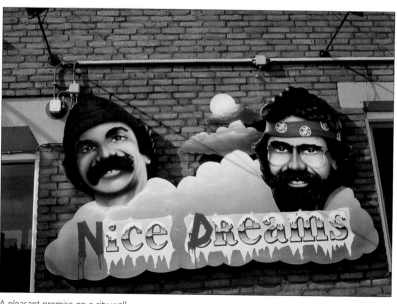

A pleasant promise on a city wall

Walking Tours

Two organisations offer interesting personalised walking tours of Amsterdam. Advance booking is essential:

Archivisie Tours tailored to your interests plus a regular programme of architectural tours.
PO Box 14603, 1001 LC Amsterdam. Tel: (020) 625 9123.

Mee in Mokum Mokum is the Yiddish name for Amsterdam; roughly translated, it means 'the place where you feel at home'. The tours are led by knowledgeable insiders, many of whom have lived in the city all their lives. *Hartenstraat 16. Tel: (020) 625 1390. Each tour is of three hours, starting 11am, Tue–Sun.*

Coach Tours

Scores of operators offer coach tours to sights which are within an hour's drive of Amsterdam, notably to the windmill museum at Zaanse Schans, the bulb fields and gardens of Lisse, the IJsselmeer villages of Volendam, Monnickendam and Marken, and the cheese markets at Alkmaar and Gouda.

Tours can be booked at any hotel through the VVV Tourist Information Office.

Pharmacies

Chemists (*drogisterij*) sell all non-prescription drugs, such as aspirin, plus toiletries, personal hygiene products, tampons and condoms. They are open only during normal shopping hours.

If you seek medical help and are given a prescription you will have to go to a pharmacy (*apotheek*) for medicines.

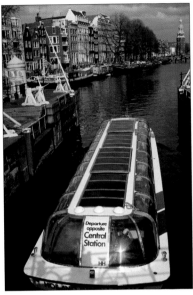

A barge on the Oude Schans Canal

These are normally open Monday to Friday 8/9am–5.30/6pm. Details of pharmacies open outside these hours are posted in all pharmacy windows and listed in the newspaper *Het Parool*. You can also phone the Central Medical Service on *(020) 592 3434*, for advice.

Places of Worship

Anglican *English Reformed Church (Engelsekerk), Begijnhof 48. Tel: (020) 624 9665.*
Roman Catholic *St John and St Ursula, Begijnhof 30. Tel: (020) 622 1918.*
Jewish (Reformed) *Jacob Soetendorpstraat 8. Tel: (020) 642 3562.*
Jewish (Orthodox) *Van der Boechorststraat 26. Tel: (020) 646 0046.*
Muslim *Kraaiennest 125. Tel: (020) 698 2526.*

Police

In emergency, telephone *112*. Otherwise, contact the Hoofdbureau Van Politie or Police Headquarters (*Elandsgracht 117; tel: (0900) 8844*) for help or advice.

Postal Services

Stamps can be bought at many tobacconists and souvenir shops. The main post office is at Singel 250–256 (*trams 1, 2, 5, 13, 14 or 17; open: Mon–Fri 9am–6pm, Thur till 8pm, Sat 10am–1.30pm*). Here you will find the full range of postal services, packaging materials on sale and telephone booths.

Poste restante mail should be addressed to the head office as follows: **Poste Restante**, *Hoofdpostkantoor PTT, Singel 250–256, 1012 SJ Amsterdam, The Netherlands.* You will need your passport as proof of identity to collect poste restante mail.

Public Transport

Amsterdam has an excellent public transport system. A free information folder, with map, is available from the GVB (Amsterdam Transport Authority) office on Stationsplein, near the Metro entrance in the same building as the VVV. You can also buy tickets here.

The system is integrated, in the sense that the same tickets are valid for tram, bus, Metro and Light Rail travel. The simplest but most expensive way of getting around is to buy a flat-fare ticket (valid for one hour) from the bus or tram driver/conductor. Alternatively, you can buy rover tickets, valid for between one and nine days, allowing unlimited use of the system.

Generally, it is advisable to buy a strip of tickets (*strippenkaart*) sold in multiples of 15 at GVB ticket counters, VVV Amsterdam Tourist Offices and tobacconists. Each ticket is valid for one hour's travel and you have to stamp one ticket for each zone you travel through, plus one.

In practice, most visitors are unlikely to travel beyond the Central Zone, so you will usually need to stamp two tickets for the journey. Fold the strip and insert the required number of units into the machines; these are located at the entrance to the Metro system, near the doors on the Light Rail or at the rear entrance doors on trams. On buses, the driver will stamp the tickets for you. Within the hour you can transfer to other buses, trams, the Metro or Light Rail so long as you stay within the same zone(s). If you get confused, other passengers are usually helpful.

Museumboot (Museumboat)

One of the most pleasant ways of travelling round Amsterdam is by the Museumboat (*tel: (020) 530 1090*). This departs every 30 (in summer) or 45 (in winter) minutes daily between 9.30am and 4.45pm from the landing stage opposite Amsterdam Centraal Station. With stops near 17 museums, it combines a canal trip with a museum visit. It makes six stops, calling at Prinsengracht, for the Anne Frank Huis, Theatremuseum and Woonboot-museum; Museum Kwartier (Museum Quarter), for the Rijksmuseum, Van Gogh Museum, Stedelijk Museum and Vondelpark; Bloemenmarkt (Flower Market), for the Bijbels Museum and

Amsterdams Historisch Museum; Waterlooplein, for Museum Het Rembrandthuis, Joods Historisch Museum, Museum Willet Holthuysen and Artis Zoo; Nautisch Kwartier (Nautical Quarter), for the Nederlands Scheepvaartmuseum and Museumwerf 't Kromhout; and back to Centraal Station, for Madame Tussaud Scenerama, Koninklijk Paleis and Museum Amstelkring.

Tickets, including day tickets giving museum discounts, can be bought from the VVV Amsterdam Tourist Office or at any landing stage.

Taxis

Should you need to use taxis in Amsterdam, you will find the drivers knowledgeable and friendly. You can try hailing a taxi in the street (a lighted sign on the roof indicates that it is free), but it is more usual to go to one of the ranks located on Stationsplein, Dam Square, the Museumplein and other well-frequented areas. Alternatively you can call the central taxi reservation number at *Taxicentrale*

(tel: (020) 677 7777). The metered fare includes a service charge but it is customary to round the fare up to the nearest euro.

Senior Citizens

Pensioners from overseas should avail themselves of discounts offered at museums and other places (*see p180*) on production of proof of status, but other discounts, on travel for example, are available only to Dutch citizens.

Sustainable tourism

Thomas Cook is a strong advocate of ethical and fairly traded tourism and believes that the travel experience should be as good for the places visited as it is for the people who visit them. That's why we firmly support The Travel Foundation: a charity that develops solutions to help improve and protect holiday destinations, their environment, traditions and culture. To find out what you can do to make a positive difference to the places you travel to and the people who live there, please visit *www.thetravelfoundation. org.uk*

AMSTERDAM
Trams &

© Communicarta Ltd, 1989-2006   UDN

Student and Youth Travel

Students are entitled to discounts on museum entry charges and on Museumcards on production of a valid student identity card or other proof of age or status.

You can eat very cheaply at one of several large subsidised student canteens (called *mensae*), which anyone can use. The most central is Mensa Atrium, Oudezijds Achterburgwal 237 (*tel: (020) 525 3999. Open: Mon–Fri, lunch noon–2pm, dinner 3–7pm*).

Accommodation in so-called 'youth hostels' is available all over the city at rock-bottom prices; you will often be approached by touts as you arrive at Amsterdam Centraal Station, and there are plenty of fly posters about advertising their services.

They can provide perfectly adequate accommodation but you should check the cleanliness before paying and ensure that your room is not located over a noisy all-night bar. You will be expected to share bedrooms and bathroom facilities with complete strangers; so trust nobody and never leave your valuables unattended.

Telephones

In all but the smaller, family-run hotels, IDD telephones are found in every room as a standard facility. The hotel charges a mark-up on the normal call rate, so you may prefer to use public facilities for overseas calls.

Public phone boxes are found throughout the city – they have a green livery and carry the green and white PTT Telecom logo. All boxes accept phonecards which can be purchased in various denominations from post offices and phone centres. Some boxes also take credit cards.

To make a call, lift the receiver, wait for the dialling tone and then insert your card. Wait till you hear a new higher tone and proceed to dial the number.

Codes

For overseas calls first dial 00 and wait for a new tone before dialling the country code (*31*) and the local code (omitting the initial *0*).

Some useful international telephone codes are listed here:

Australia *61.*
Ireland *353.*
New Zealand *64.*
UK *44.*
USA and Canada *1.*

The code for Amsterdam is *020;* if you are dialling from abroad omit the initial zero.

Local Operator *0800 0101.*
International Operator *0800 0410.*
International Directory Enquiries *0900 8418.*
National Directory Enquiries *0900 8008.*

Phone Centres

At some centres, you can make as many calls as you like and pay afterwards with cash, credit card, traveller's cheque or Eurocheque. You can send faxes and telexes, and purchase phonecards, too. A telephone card may also be obtained from the PTT post offices.

Time
Amsterdam observes Central European Time, which is one hour ahead of Greenwich Mean Time in winter and two hours ahead from late March to late October.

Tipping
A service charge is automatically included in the prices on restaurant menus and in metered taxi fares. Despite that, you are expected to tip about 5–10 per cent of the bill in a restaurant, and 10 per cent for a taxi ride – but do this only if you are satisfied with the service.

Toilets
Old-fashioned urinals for men dot Amsterdam. Women may have to resort to buying a drink in a café in order to make use of their toilets. There are also clean facilities in museums, restaurants, cafés and department stores.

Tourist Information
The Netherlands has an excellent network of Tourist Information Offices where the standard of service is extremely high. Their official title is Vereniging Voor Vreemdelingenverkeer – the Association for Tourist Traffic – universally abbreviated to the initials VVV (pronounced *Fay Fay Fay*).

Offices are found near the station or main square in every town or city in the country. In Amsterdam the main office is located opposite Centraal Station (Stationsplein 10; *tel: 0900 400 4040, for information at 55 cents per minute;* open daily 9am–5pm). This office provides a wide range of services in addition to information and advice. It also sells its own listings magazine, *What's On in Amsterdam*, a range of maps and leaflets, and it operates a bureau de change.

There is another office inside Centraal Station and branches at Leidseplein and Argonautenstraat (near Stadioplein) (all open daily). At Schiphol airport, Holland Tourist Information (open: daily 7am–10pm) is helpful for incoming visitors who require information and bookings. Outside the country, branches of The Netherlands Board of Tourism can also be found in most capital cities: Some of the locations are given below:

Australia
5 Elizabeth Street,
Suite 302, Sydney, NSW 2000.
Tel: (02) 247 6921.

Canada
25 Adelaide Street East, Suite 710,
Toronto, ON M5C 1Y2.
Tel: 416 363 1577.

Traditional blue and white tiles

UK
PO Box 30783, London WC2B 6DH.
Tel: (020) 7539 7950.
USA
355 Lexington Avenue, 19th Floor, New York, NY 10017. Tel: 1-888-2-HOLLAND.

Travellers with Disabilities

Steep hotel staircases and broken pavements are the main hazards facing travellers with disabilities. Otherwise Amsterdam has an enlightened policy towards people with special needs, and most museums, cinemas and theatres have wheelchair access and adapted toilets.

Brochures issued by The Netherlands Board of Tourism and VVV Tourist Information Centres give information that includes details of hotels and tourist attractions with access and facilities for people with disabilities.

Trams are impossible to use with a wheelchair because of high steps but there are lifts in all Metro stations except for Waterlooplein, and there is a special taxi service for wheelchair users. (*Tel: (020) 633 3943, office hours Mon–Fri 7am–5pm, advance booking essential.*)

In Amsterdam, you can obtain information or report a problem you think needs addressing by contacting the English-speaking staff of SGOA – the Stichting Gehandicapten Overleg Amsterdam (*Quellijnstraat 89; tel: (020) 577 7955; open: Mon–Fri 9am–5pm*), an organisation that works to improve facilities for people with disabilities.

Amsterdam's waterfront tourist office

ACKNOWLEDGEMENTS
Thomas Cook Publishing wishes to thank the following photographers, libraries and associations for their assistance in the preparation of this book, and to whom the copyright belongs.
EDDY POSTHUMA DE BOER 2, 3, 5, 6, 7, 10, 11, 12, 13, 14, 15, 16, 17, 19, 20, 22, 23b, 26, 27, 32, 33, 34, 39, 44a, 44b, 45a, 45b, 46a, 46b, 48, 49a, 50a, 51a, 51b, 55, 58, 59, 62, 63, 65, 71, 72, 74, 75b, 79, 80, 81, 82, 84, 85, 90, 91, 92, 93a, 93b, 94a, 95a, 98, 100, 101, 102, 103, 104, 105, 106, 107, 108, 111, 112, 113, 114, 115, 116, 118, 119, 121, 122, 123, 124, 126, 127, 128, 129, 130, 134, 135, 138b, 139a, 145a, 145b, 156, 157, 158b, 159, 160a, 160b, 161a, 161b, 168b, 169a, 169b, 179
MIKE GERRARD 138, 176
PICTURES COLOUR LIBRARY 61, 68, 110, 167
PLANET WARE 60
www.bigfoto.com 144

The remaining pictures are held in the AA PHOTO LIBRARY and were taken by: KEN PATERSON with the exception of pages 35, 50b, 54, 73, 83, 88a, 94b, 95b, 131, 136, 137, 138a, 139b, 140, 141, 146a, 146b, 147, 150, 154, 158a, 162, 164, 165, 166, 168a, 170a, 170b, 171, 173, 174, 177, 181, 182, 188 which were taken by WYN VOYSEY.

Index: MARIE LORIMER
Proof reading: GAYNOR SPRY for CAMBRIDGE PUBLISHING MANAGEMENT LIMITED

Travellers Amsterdam

Feedback Form

Please help us improve future editions by taking part in our reader survey. Every returned form will be acknowledged. To show our appreciation we will send you a voucher entitling you to £1 off your next *Travellers* guide or any other Thomas Cook guidebook ordered direct from Thomas Cook Publishing. Just take a few minutes to complete and return this form to us.

We'd also be glad to hear of your comments, updates or recommendations on places we cover or you think that we ought to cover.

1. Which of the following tempted you into buying your *Travellers* guide:
   (Please tick as many as appropriate)

   a) the price ☐

   b) the cover ☐

   c) the content ☐

   d) other _____

2. What do you think of:

   a) the cover design _____

   b) the design and layout styles within the book _____

   c) the content_____

   d) the maps _____

3. Please tell us about any features that in your opinion could be changed, improved or added in future editions of the book or any other comments you would like to make concerning this book _____

   _____

   _____

   _____

   _____

4. What is the single most useful/helpful aspect of this book?_____

   _____

5. Have you purchased other *Travellers* guides in the series?

a) yes ☐

b) no ☐

If yes, please specify which titles _____

6. Would you purchase other *Travellers* guides?

a) yes ☐

b) no ☐

If no, please specify why not _____

Your age category: ☐ under 21   ☐ 21–30   ☐ 31–40   ☐ 41–50   ☐ 51+

Mr/Mrs/Miss/Ms/Other

Surname_____ Initials_____

Full address (please include postal or zip code):_____

_____

_____

Daytime telephone number: _____

E-mail address:_____

Please detach this page and send it to: **The Series Editor,** *Travellers* **guides,
Thomas Cook Publishing, PO Box 227, The Thomas Cook Business Park,
Units 15–16, Coningsby Road, Peterborough PE3 8SB, United Kingdom.**

Alternatively, you can e-mail us at: *books@thomascook.com*